Georgian London

Derek Brechin

Picture sources: Mansell Collection, pp. 28, 89; Radio Times Hulton Picture Library, pp. 11, 15, 19, 25, 32, 35, 39, 45, 47, 55, 58, 60, 62, 69, 75, 77, 83, 87. Photographs in centre section: Stanley Devon, from *Royal Greenwich* 1, 5, 7; Radio Times Hulton Picture Library 2; Michael Taylor 3, 4, 6, 8. Guildhall Museum slipcase illustration.

SBN 356 02567 5

First published in 1969 by
Macdonald & Co. (Publishers) Ltd.
St. Giles House, 49 Poland St., London W.1

Reprinted 1969

Made and printed in Great Britain by
Purnell & Sons Ltd., Paulton, Somerset

Discovering London 6

Georgian London

Derek Brechin

Macdonald : London

Contents

Cover: a perspective view of the Bank of England building, completed in 1734.

Slipcase illustration: Visscher's panorama of London, 1616.

Introduction

This book is the sixth in the *Discovering London* series. It deals with the period from the Glorious Revolution of 1688, which removed James II from the throne, to the accession of George III, the third of the Hanoverian line.

The reigns of William and Mary, Anne, George I and George II witnessed a burst of activity at home and abroad—activity which led to the Industrial Revolution at home and the foundation of the British Empire abroad. Its prosperity was reflected in the stately homes of the long-established and newly established rich, and by the fleets of merchant ships jamming the Thames. But at the other end of the scale, the poor—particularly in London—suffered even greater deprivation and hardship than ever before. The newly laid out spacious squares in London's West End stand in vivid contrast to the over-crowded tenements and hovels further east. Grace on the one hand, squalor on the other—that is the picture of the expanded and ever-expanding London of the period.

Prelude: The Georgian Philosophy of Life

'Nature and Nature's Laws lay hid in Night:
God said, let Newton be! and all was light.'

Sir Isaac Newton had in the previous century established the existence of an ordered universe. This achievement was to have a much wider effect than merely in the world of physical science; it was to influence and dominate the entire Georgian way of life. Not only did it stimulate an interest in science itself, in scientific experiment and research, which was to lay the foundations of the Industrial Revolution, but it coloured and directed man's intellectual thought towards a reconsideration of himself. If the entire universe was ordered, obeying a few immutable rules, surely man too (an object in nature) was similarly ordered. All one had to do was (following Newton's rational method) to collect the facts, study them and discover the laws which govern human thought and emotion. Then, not only would man's psychology be revealed, but every sphere of human activity would be understandable, and when understood, perfectable—social and political relations, aesthetics and morals. The Age of Reason was under way, and the perfect society, Utopia, seemed attainable at last. 'All was light', and the new age went on its way with a self-confidence which it is hard to find in any other period. It accounts for the enormous strides made in the 18th century, leaving the Middle Ages far behind and ending with at least one foot in the door of modern times.

We shall see throughout the book how the rational scientific outlook with its contingent optimism colours every sphere of 18th-century life, usually with the expected positive results, but occasionally, as in its attitude towards the poor, with less happy ones.

England after the Glorious Revolution

The Glorious (because bloodless) Revolution of 1688, which limited the power of the crown (especially that of suspending Parliament), and the Act of Settlement of 1701, which strengthened the power of Parliament, went a great way to sounding the death knell of the Divine Right of Kings.

Not only in 1688 was a king quickly removed and another (not the immediate heir) set on the throne, but the running of the country was to be shared between Parliament and a 'salaried king' whose religion (Church of England) was fixed for him.

The balance of power and the exact roles of king and Parliament were, at this stage, left undefined, but the 'working arrangement' was weighted by this constitutional revolution in favour of Parliament and the Cabinet (the name given to a small body of Privy Councillors summoned regularly for consultation by the sovereign). Cabinet meetings under the first two Georges led to the evolution of a leading minister. The role of Prime Minister emerged at first unofficially. Walpole may be seen as the first Prime Minister, but only in the sense that his leadership was recognised (if not always approved of on constitutional grounds) by his fellow members of Parliament; he was not a Prime Minister in the modern sense, a leader of the majority party and head of the ministry. The first Prime Minister to be actually given the title was Pitt the Younger. Nor did parties have the significance they have today; Whigs and Tories were loosely grouped bodies rather than tightly disciplined divisions.

In brief, the king was head of the state, choosing his ministers and determining policies, but he could no longer do so with a free hand. The ministers he chose had to have control of the Commons since his policies depended on the voting of the necessary finances. So the 'Prime Minister' was to some extent a middle-man, working between the two centres of power, the Crown and the Commons.

The business of a Prime Minister, then, was to make sure he could rely on parliamentary support without a majority party. His main tool was 'influence', which he exerted over the body of independent country gentlemen who made up half the membership of the Commons, and over the 'placemen', the non-'party' men who always voted for the king's government.

The term 'Commons' was something of a misnomer at the time, for the members were nearly all drawn from the aristocracy and the gentry, elected with great ease from the 'pocket' boroughs (constituencies they had in their pockets) and 'rotten' boroughs, where the few votes were sold to the highest bidder. The Duke of Newcastle by these means controlled no less than fifty seats in the House of Commons and no cabinet between 1725 and 1761 was complete without him. There was no secret ballot; votes were cast openly, so voters could be 'pressurised' where necessary. Sometimes it wasn't necessary, or at least not on voting day itself. 'I was unanimously elected by one Elector', wrote one member. 'There was no other Candidate, no Opposition, no Poll demanded, Security or Petition.' But obviously this was an exceptional case; in a larger electorate, 'influence', speech-making and other more modern campaigning devices had to be employed alongside bribery and forcible persuasion.

Such a system can, and naturally has, been criticised. But there is no doubt that, corrupt though it was, it provided a stable government, and its aristocratic and business-dominated structure was well suited to the economic explosion which was under way, sparked off by better farming at home and trade expansion abroad.

The Wars Abroad

It is often hard to remember when reading social histories of the England of William and Mary, Anne and George I and II that the country was at war for much of the period. The atmosphere seems so full of self-assurance, confidence and well-being, so lacking in doubt or anxiety, that war seems far from the scene. And so it was in a sense. War was a foreign affair; the country itself was touched by it only incidentally, generally through the pocket. After the conflict of the Civil War, the relatively peaceful situation which followed the Glorious Revolution was extremely welcome. The wars which form a distant background to the post-Revolution scene were largely mercantile. Their aim was to protect and extend trade abroad; they did not involve a bitter struggle between Englishman and Englishman. On the few occasions when civil unrest returned to the land—notably the '15 and '45 rebellions by the Old and Young Pretenders—old fires were fanned and old fears of Stuart tyranny were reawakened, but these upheavals were few and far between and of no great duration. They were single gunshots momentarily shattering the peace of a long sunny day.

East India House, Leadenhall Street, the headquarters of the East India Company, whose trade contributed greatly to the growing prosperity of the City in Georgian times.

In 1742, Walpole, who had successfully kept England out of war for nearly 20 years, resigned. In 1757, England's greatest war leader until Winston Churchill, William Pitt, arrived on the scene. The darling of the people, particularly of the City of London, whose commercial interests the war naturally protected and in the long run improved, Pitt led the country to triumph. By 1760, the end of our period, Britain was a world power, dominating the seas and, thanks to Clive and Wolfe, controlling India and Canada. In that year, the foundation stone of the new Blackfriars Bridge was laid, dedicated to Pitt. It was 'a monument to the city's affection to the man who by the strength of his genius and the steadfastness of his mind and a certain kind of happy contagion of his probity and spirit recovered, augmented and secured the British Empire in Asia, Africa and America and restored the ancient reputation and influence of this country amongst the nations of Europe'.

Home Affairs

It has been suggested that the slogan 'business as usual', often used to describe the situation at home during the 1914–18 War, applies equally to the period of the Glorious Revolution and later. Certainly business was the main preoccupation. Not that the events abroad went unnoticed or victories uncelebrated. After the English and Dutch fleets had prevented invasion by Louis XIV by winning the Battle of La Hogue, 'during seven days the bells of London pealed without ceasing. Flags were flying on all the steeples. Rows of candles were in all the windows. Bonfires were at all the corners of the streets. And three lords took down with them £37,000 in coin to distribute among the sailors'. A more permanent token of gratitude was provided by William III; he converted the Royal Palace at Greenwich into a hospital to the design of Sir Christopher Wren, who gave his services free.

Two permanent legacies of William's wars are the National Debt and the Bank of England, founded in 1693, mainly to raise more funds for them. Several money-raising schemes had already been considered in the City, which naturally backed the wars in the interest of trade expansion, before a syndicate was formed, headed by the Scotsman William Paterson, to lend the vast sum of £1,200,000 to the government on the security of certain import duties. The syndicate was incorporated under the name of the Bank of England by an Act of Parliament, which also laid down that no other bank could obtain a charter. According to the historian Bernard Ash the bank became the 'purse of the government' and 'the whole machinery of the National Debt came into existence, the foundation of modern government finance was laid'.

Despite the Bank of England's monopoly, other banks succeeded in establishing themselves, most of which gained their charters for ostensible manufacturing purposes rather than the actual banking of money. One of these, the Sword Blade Bank, was the instigator of the notorious South Sea Bubble, which after deliberate inflation to attract the gambling-crazed populace overextended itself and finally burst in 1720. It left the Bank of England still in business, and many investors very much out of it, so great were the losses. The affluent and the not so affluent were both attracted by such get-rich-quick schemes, which were one of the main ways of improving one's financial, and so social, position.

Class Structure

'Fate has but little Distinction set
Betwixt the Counter and the Coronet.'

The lines are Daniel Defoe's; they imply that movement between the classes was reasonably free, at least between the middle and the upper. This was largely true, but if the statement is extended to include movement upward from the very lowest scale it requires qualification. Or at least it requires the exceptional man. It was possible for the Joe Lampton of the time to get to the top. The Industrial Revolution later in the century, for example, offered opportunities to men of talent and enterprise, such as the yeoman Robert Peel and the barber Richard Arkwright, who were quick to seize them. But even a barber was well up the social scale compared with the majority of London's poor and among them it was the rare man indeed who could raise himself up out of his dingy cellar.

Nevertheless, though the social ladder was long and the steps up it were many, these steps were placed closer together than ever before, and virtually equidistant at all points. And between the bottom and the top the swelling middle classes were already subdividing themselves into lower-middle, middle-middle and upper-middle. It isn't always easy now to see the joins, where one class ended and where the next began, but doubtless at the time the labels were very clearly attached.

But if society was class-conscious, it was not rigidly caste ridden and the climber was quickly accepted in his new position. The only requirement was the necessary amount of money; it didn't matter too much how you'd made it—by clever speculation, a judicious marriage or exploitation—the important thing was to have it.

The Upper Classes

The more money you had, the more you could make. The greatest source of revenue in Georgian times was land; those who already had plenty were clearly in the best position to make money from it and add to it. Consequently they bought out the smaller landowners and extended their estates. It was a case of the established

A gentleman wearing the court dress of 1760 in front of St. James's Palace.

establishing themselves even more securely—and more ostentatiously; the main aim of the large estate with the grand family mansion was to display the family's social and political eminence.

The stately home was also a political power house, as we have seen. Political power and money walked hand in hand, palm to itchy palm. More of one led to more of the other. The roll of members of the House of Commons read like a list of the top families. Fathers got their sons into the House as soon as they were of age, since public service was the best means of accumulating more wealth for the family coffers. Before entering the government, Sir Robert Walpole had an estate worth about £2000 a year. In a handful of years his house was torn down to make way for a palace; after 21 years as 'Prime Minister' his art collection alone was worth £40,000. Political prestige (and its concomitant wealth) was the goal aimed for by those who bought land with the proceeds from investment in business.

The country was still basically an agricultural community; the leaders of society were still essentially countrymen, to whom London was the place to go to only in 'the season', which corresponded with the parliamentary term. But 'the season' was a busy one, not only because the aristocrats now controlled the central government as well as local affairs, but because their money-making activities involved them with big business and the commercial world of the city. Here they would mingle with the new breed, the middle classes.

The Middle Classes

'The Commerce of England is an immense and almost incredible thing'; 'Our Merchants are Princes greater and richer and more powerful than some sovereign Princes'. Defoe again, and writing as he did at the beginning of the 18th century, there is little doubt (though he was in trade himself at the time) that he is right in stressing the activity and achievements of the new businessmen. (Defoe, in fact, had his finger firmly on the pulse of the country; the conditions he lays the most stress on in his *Tour through Great Britain* are precisely those which led ultimately to the Industrial Revolution, as yet a wisp of smoke on the tree-lined horizon.)

A great business era was indeed under way and some certainly raised themselves to princely level. London was the centre of course, though sea-faring England could boast a tycoon in every port. These merchants would deal with internal trade, despatching their goods by water, either by sea or river. (Transport was still largely by water, since the roads were still in a shocking condition.) They also dealt in foreign trade to and from all corners of the world—tea from China, grindstones to Sweden, tobacco from Virginia resold to Russia, sugar from the West Indies and English cloth to every land. If the Roman Empire was built on military pride, the British Empire was founded by ambitious trading.

The successful merchant took several rungs of the ladder in his stride, and having studied and aped its way of life from below, was soon accepted on an equal footing by the upper class.

Below him, the middle-middle and the lower-middle classes—the shopkeepers and wholesalers, the lawyers and the civil servants—grew as the towns grew. Here the movement upward was in many cases a general one, produced less by individual ambition and achievement than by acquiring a new and generally recognised status. Trades became professions. Perhaps the first professional figure to acquire the new standing was the architect, but he was quickly followed by those in the lesser branches of the law, the medical man and the civil servant. The professions so established formed a new rung on the ladder midway between the trader and the gentry. So the climb from half-way up the ladder was all the time becoming easier, although the distance from bottom to middle remained as great, if not greater. Even so, the middle classes, growing as they were, did not occupy the important position they were to have later. They did not see themselves as a class with an ideology of their own; bourgeois values only evolved when the avenue to the top was closed. In Georgian times, the middle class was a temporary stop on the way up. Consequently they were happy to adopt the values of their betters, to ape their manners and copy their furniture, to attain instant gentility by an avid reading of Lord Chesterfield's letters to his son on the importance of good manners. It made for good business; a business man, writing to his son recommending Chesterfield, advised him 'you may be assured if you add to the little learning and improvement you have hitherto had, the Manner, the Air, the genteel address and polite behaviour of a gentleman, you will abundantly find [reward] in it, in all and every transaction of your future life—when you come to do business in the World'. It was not just a matter of cultivating the rich in order to take their money from them; the ability to mingle with them in their own manner was a necessary social accomplishment. Patronage was the key that turned the lock to political and therefore social and financial advancement. How to win friends among people with influence was the text of the day for the 'middling sort of people'.

The Working Classes and the Poor

'And when they were up they were up
And when they were down they were down.'

Not Defoe this time but the rhyme about the Grand Old Duke of York, summing up for us the enormous gap between the top and the bottom. The climb was possible,

Typical Londoners at the time of William and Mary.

as we have pointed out. In one of the greatest gambling ages we have known anything was possible—the downward fall as well as the climb. But the game was snakes and ladders and the climb usually took longer than the fall. And if you couldn't even afford the dice you couldn't get in on the game at all.

Unfortunately this was all too often true, among countrymen and townsmen alike, but nowhere was it more true than among the London poor, as we shall see when we come to take a look at life in the cities of London and Westminster. At this point, however, it is well to stress that we must be careful not to think of the poor as one large mass all of equal poverty. The subtle distinction of the Georgian class structure existed among the poor too—distinctions clung to with a fiercer pride than further up the ladder. At this level, the bottom rung was the standard of comparison not the top; the fear of moving downwards was greater than the need to climb upwards.

Though the Industrial Revolution itself was to affect it perhaps less than other parts of the country, London was already full of light industries as well as the older trades, carried on at home (by the domestic system) and in small workshops. Such trades included coach-building, sign painting, silk-weaving and in particular watch- and clock-making, for which London was world famous at the time.

But the subdivisions of class were seen not only in the enormous variety of trades and industries themselves, but more revealingly in housing conditions. In London, as elsewhere, the great test of status was whether or not one was a 'housekeeper' or householder. In the main, these would be shopkeepers or better-off artisans. They would live, man, wife and family not in the whole house but in one or two rooms only. The other rooms would be let out furnished (if that is not too grand a description) at a weekly rent, and the position of the room in the house firmly established the status of the person renting it. The poorest class occupied the cellar or the garret where, according to a contemporary source, 'from three to eight individuals of different ages often slept in the same bed, there being in general about one room and one bed for each family'. 'From thence', comments another writer of the time in a more flippant, yet still accurate manner, 'we gradually descend to the second and first floor, the dignity of each being in the reverse ratio of its altitude, it being always remembered that those dwelling in the forepart of the house take the "pas" of the inhabitants of the back rooms, and the ground floor, if not a shop and warehouse, ranks with the second story.' But there were many who did not live even in the furnished cellars of householders at a weekly rent; lodging houses charging twopence a night began to spring up at the start of the 18th century and, further down the scale still, was the shed dwelling commonest on the outskirts of London.

From the shed to the stately home was a long journey and the road (like the actual roads of the time) was full of pitfalls. So, although it was, in theory, possible to follow the road from the bottom to the top, it was usually true to say that 'when they were down they were down'.

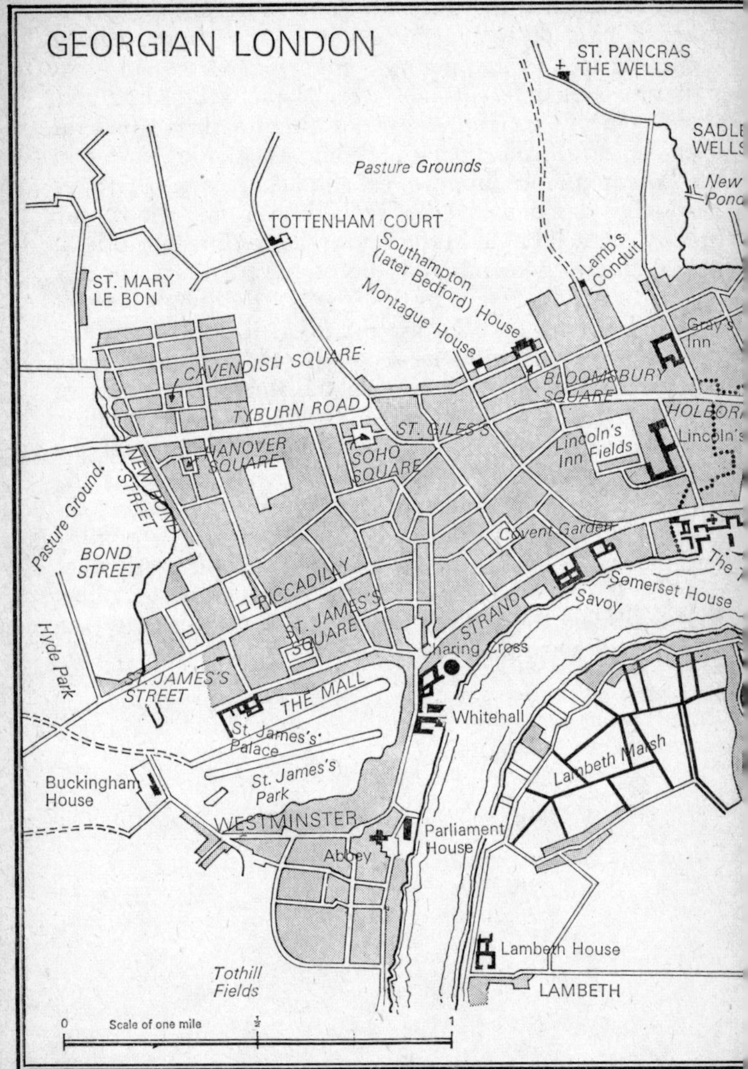
GEORGIAN LONDON
ST. PANCRAS
THE WELLS
Pasture Grounds
TOTTENHAM COURT
Southampton (later Bedford) House
Montague House
Lamb's Conduit
ST. MARY LE BON
CAVENDISH SQUARE
BLOOMSBURY SQUARE
TYBURN ROAD
ST. GILES'S
Lincoln's Inn Fields
HANOVER SQUARE
SOHO SQUARE
NEW BOND STREET
Pasture Ground.
BOND STREET
Covent Garden
PICCADILLY
Somerset House
Savoy
ST. JAMES'S SQUARE
STRAND
Charing Cross
Hyde Park
ST. JAMES'S STREET
THE MALL
Whitehall
St. James's Palace
St. James's Park
Buckingham House
Lambeth Marsh
WESTMINSTER
Parliament House
Abbey
Lambeth House
Tothill Fields
LAMBETH
0
Scale of one mile
½
1

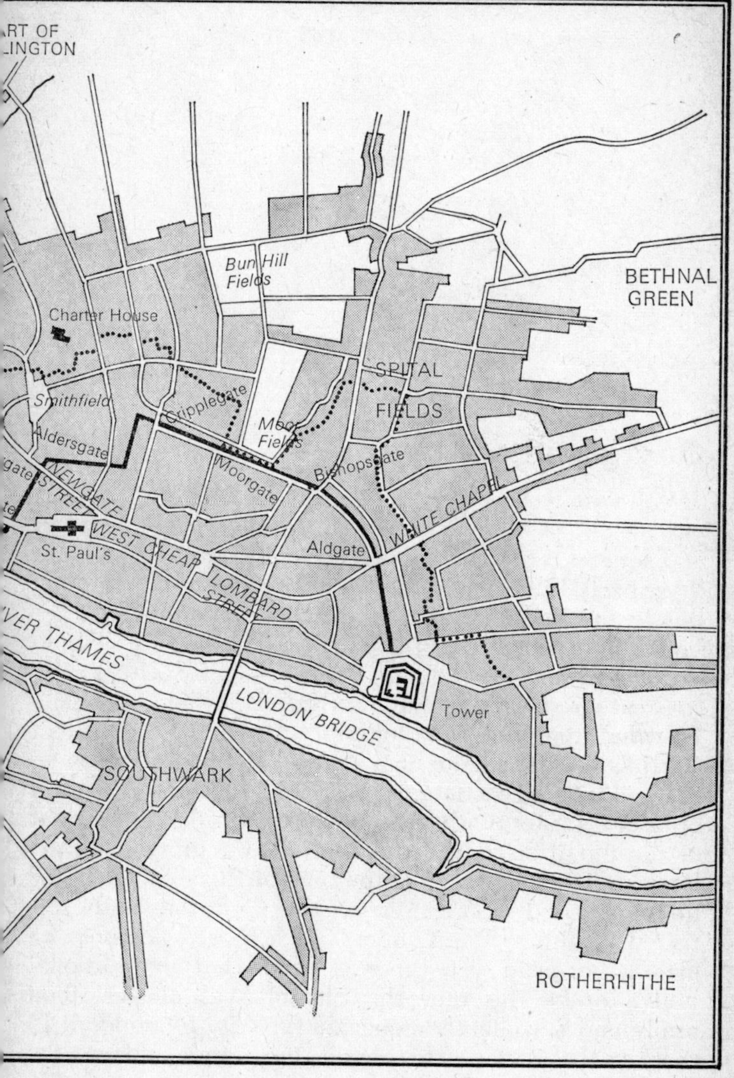
BETHNAL GREEN
Bun Hill Fields
Charter House
SPITAL FIELDS
Smithfield
Cripplegate
Moor Fields
Aldersgate
Moorgate
Bishopsgate
NEWGATE STREET
WHITE CHAPEL
WEST CHEAP
St. Paul's
Aldgate
LOMBARD STREET
LONDON BRIDGE
Tower
SOUTHWARK
ROTHERHITHE

Georgian London

'If you wish to have a just notion of the magnitude of this city, you must not be satisfied with seeing its great streets and squares, but must survey the innumerable little lanes and courts. It is not in the showy evolution of building, but in the multiplicity of human habitations which are crowded together, that the wonderful immensity of London consists.'

Great streets and squares . . . little lanes and courts . . . crowded together—Dr Johnson gives us an excellent starting point to set out on a tour of Georgian London.

London, already described by an earlier observer as 'a kind of monster, with a head enormously large, and out of all proportion to its body', continued to grow along the lines already evident from the time of Elizabeth I. These lines extended outwards from the City, the 'body' referred to above. But London had acquired not only an even larger head (if not indeed 'heads') but an additional body, for by this time the City of Westminster stood firmly and corpulently alongside the City of London. In fact, at the start of our period, the square mile of the

A condemned criminal on his way to execution fainting on the arrival of a reprieve. The journey from Newgate to Tyburn was three miles along streets lined with jeering crowds.

City was only about a fifth part of the area occupied by the metropolis of Greater London.

According to foreign travellers like Cesar de Sausure, who visited the capital in 1727, London had a population of about a million and stretched ten miles along the river and three miles from north to south, including the river. However, both these statistics need correcting. It is doubtful if the population was more than 650,000 and not all of the area mentioned was by that time built-up. The ten-mile stretch must have been meant to include, for example, the 'villages' west of Pimlico, although of these not even Chelsea was yet properly joined to the metropolis.

This, the built-up area of the metropolis, is shown in a map by Bowe (1723) to extend along the river from Wapping to Horseferry in Westminster; from there the boundary ran north to Tyburn Road (Oxford Street) via Buckingham Gate, St. James's Street, Old and New Bond Street, turned east along the lines of Oxford Street, Theobalds Road, Old Street and City Road, and returned towards the river via Houndsditch and the Minories.

On John Rocque's maps of the 1740s, the built-up area has expanded to include Pimlico on the west and Shadwell on the east; to the north the city has spread beyond Moorfields and the Artillery Ground and to the north-west into Marylebone, although this area was still largely countryside, with Marylebone Road no more than a foot-path. South of the river, Southwark was slowly growing, but further west Lambeth was still undeveloped and remained so until well after the opening of Westminster Bridge in 1750—in fact, until the end of the century, when new roads were built connecting it with the Elephant and Castle.

In general, London grew outwards in long lines, following existing roads, while the space between the lines gradually came to be filled in. The new roads built later in the century encouraged the same sort of building as well as opening up new areas for development. But until roads attained a higher standard of construction and upkeep the 'village' pattern persisted, not only outside the metropolis but inside as well. The difficulty of travelling about the city was almost as great a reason for the self-contained communities of early 18th-century London as the more obvious one of class consciousness. Whichever way you looked at it, the distance from London's East End to the West End was vast. In the east were 'narrow, dark and ill-paved streets', wrote another foreign visitor. 'The contrast between this and the West End is astonishing: the houses here are mostly new and elegant; the squares are superb, the streets straight and open.'

The West End

Great Queen Street, 'the first regular street in London', and Bloomsbury Square, the first square in London to actually be given the name 'square', were already in existence before our period begins. In fact, they were there before the Plague, which encouraged the movement westwards from the previously fashionable area around Aldwych, brought about by the desire of the wealthy to 'live windward of noxious vapours'. The Fire, the following year, stimulated the development of a more spacious dwelling area.

So by the beginning of the 18th century, Soho, Gray's Inn and the West End had been well developed by speculators whose names often live on in the streets they built—Panton, Jermyn and Frith, for example. St. James's Square was the centre of the fashionable world. The development of the West End slowed down somewhat about the start of George I's reign, but by the time Rocque made his maps the western extremity was Park Lane and the whole area between Oxford Street and Piccadilly had been laid out in 'superb squares' and 'straight open streets'. Moreover the fashionable move

A London lamplighter (based on a drawing by Hogarth) replenishing a wick with oil.

westwards continued; Covent Garden (in fact the first London square, though it was not called so) and the areas round St. Giles and Soho (also with its square, then called King Square) were deserted in favour of Hanover, Grosvenor, Portman and Cavendish Squares, though the last two were slower to develop than the area south of Oxford Street, perhaps because of the distance from Westminster.

The East End

In contrast to the well-planned, long-lease buildings of the West End, London's East End grew in a haphazard fashion. The 'lines' had spread out from the City as far as Mile End, Stepney and into Bethnal Green, and by the time of Rocque's maps, the area's development into densely built urban communities, houses crowded into rambling areas of narrow streets, courts and windy alleys, with common sewers flowing through the centres, was already under way. Nearer the City, and precipitating the need for the further expansion eastwards, was Spitalfields, which had been built over earlier as a result of the great influx of Huguenot refugees after the revocation of the Edict of Nantes in 1685. Here they settled and established London's important silk-weaving industry.

Refugees and immigrants, Jews and Irishmen in particular, uprooted countrymen, and vagrants from all parts of the land—to these London was a magnet, often a last hope. In an effort to stop the immigration and halt the growth of London, attempts had been made in the previous century (and earlier) to prevent the construction of the new buildings needed to house the new arrivals, who were mainly poor. These restrictions failed to stem the flow; what they did achieve was further expansion and the conversion of London into a place 'where falling houses thunder on your head'. Since brand-new houses were prohibited, the old houses had to be patched up anyhow and additions, like the digging of cellars, made to them for extra accommodation. When the regulations were defied and new buildings were put up, they were tucked away behind existing façades, hidden in yards, and naturally, with detection and demolition likely, were simply thrown together in a ramshackle, temporary way. Such building became a habit, even after the restrictions had been lifted. There were few large houses in the East. Such as there had been, for example, in Bethnal Green, formerly the country-house area of City merchants, were now dilapidated, the owners having moved westwards as the houses of the poor moved in.

Ramshackle building, overcrowding, poverty—these were the characteristics of the East End, seen at their worst in the older areas nearer the City walls.

The City

With the rise of Westminster both as a centre of power and consequently of the fashionable world, the City began to lose some of its former importance. Although it regained some ground in the second half of the century, the City Fathers of the early years seemed to consider it more important to maintain its ancient position as an independent state than to extend its power to include the administration of the new territories developing outside its old walls. Perhaps this is understandable after the undermining of the traditional rights by James II, but it was nevertheless short-sighted to strengthen the city walls, which is what was done both literally (up to the mid-century) and metaphorically. So while the new suburbs sprang up around it, organising themselves into parochial governments, the City wanted nothing to do with them and preferred an inward-looking policy. Yet even this policy failed to let it see what was going on within the walls themselves—that there was an outward movement of some of its own inhabitants. Many goldsmiths, for example, had already deserted the City for new shops in the Strand. At the same time the new style of financier moved in, and proceeded to work outside the control of the Corporation, and live outside the City itself. Although the City was not yet a place of business by day deserted by night, as it is today, we can nonetheless see the first beginnings of the commuter.

Yet, despite its loss of status and power in the metropolis, the City was as prosperous as ever, if not more so, particularly as a result of its new role in world finance. Its hero was Pitt, who gave it a trading empire. Its policy, inward-looking as regards political power, was decidedly outward-looking as regards money.

The River

The Thames was a busy colourful waterway growing busier daily. At the start of our period it carried some 15,000 small boats and ferries as well as the barges of the rich merchants and livery companies above London's only bridge. And lower down, it almost disappeared from sight under the countless 'merchant vessels from every country anchored in rows'. Apart from the increased traffic on its waters, the river was little changed from the previous century. Riverside villas and green meadows still lined its banks all the way from Richmond to the Strand. Battersea, for example, was still famous for its market gardens and its skyline was still unblotted by the factory smoke which appears hanging over it in a print of 1752.

Just before this print was made, the face of the river itself was changed by the construction of a bridge at Westminster. Work had begun in 1738 and the bridge was opened in 1750. (This Westminster Bridge, the inspiration of Wordsworth's famous sonnet, was replaced in the mid-19th century by the present one.) It was about

A hawker of river water in the streets of London. Water from the Thames was highly polluted—one of the reasons for the widespread drinking of alcohol.

40 feet across, twice as wide as London Bridge and its broader arches allowed more than four times as much space for river traffic.

The building of the new bridge in rival Westminster stung the City Fathers into action. At first they didn't go as far as actually building another bridge; they contented themselves with trying to ensure that old London Bridge would not fall down by removing all the houses on it. The broader carriageway thus provided certainly helped to solve the traffic problem, but it was no real solution. So, in 1760, the much discussed new bridge, Blackfriars, was finally got under way. Blackfriars Bridge (again not the present bridge, which is a reconstruction of the 1860s, widened in the 1900s) not only eased the flow of traffic over the river and opened up new areas for development, it also caused the disappearance of the Fleet River or ditch as it then was. Fleet Ditch had been filled in as far south as Holborn Bridge in the 1730s. In 1765, with the laying of the approaches to Blackfriars Bridge, the remainder of the lava-like stream of garbage, its banks lined with tottering latrines, was covered over. (The Fleet still flows from Hampstead to the Thames, its final section via a sewer under Farringdon Street and New Bridge Street.)

The New Face of London

By the end of our period then, London had two new bridges as well as a new West End and new suburbs. If it can be said to have a characteristic face it was one carved out by Wren: his churches were to be seen all over the City dominated by the finally complete new St. Paul's Cathedral; in City and suburb alike his influence was stamped on domestic architecture and in the realm of public building his own work was widespread—the Royal Hospitals of Chelsea and Greenwich, Morden College at Blackheath, Marlborough House in Pall Mall, the extension to St. James's Palace and Kensington Palace. This last building shows how the monarchy influenced the growth of London—build a palace and a fashionable suburb was almost bound to develop around it, as Kensington and Knightsbridge did. Not immediately of course; until the end of the 18th century Kensington remained a village and the palace with its new orangery could have been seldom visited by sightseers from the heart of London. William and Mary also made great changes at Hampton Court, including the planting of the famous maze.

Queen Anne expanded the grounds of Kensington Palace by annexing some of Hyde Park. Later, George II's wife, Caroline, wanted to annexe the whole of the park, but was dissuaded from this by Walpole and contented herself with about 250 acres within which she had the Serpentine constructed.

In Queen Anne's reign an Act of Parliament provided for the building of fifty new churches 'in or around the Cities of London and Westminster or the Suburbs thereof'. In fact only a dozen came to be built, some in the two cities, some as far afield as Gravesend. More churches did spring up in many districts, not raised by Parliamentary grant but by subscriptions by local inhabitants, jealous of the new buildings in neighbouring areas. Examples of these can be found at Richmond, Twickenham and Hampstead.

Meanwhile the City was stirring itself to a realisation of the importance of acquiring an appearance more fitting to its new international status. In 1734, after carrying on its business without a proper base for 40 years, the Bank of England moved into its own building in Threadneedle Street. The original building was much smaller than the present one, but by the 1790s it took over all the 'island' on which it now stands and was frequently extended and reconstructed until its completion in 1833. In 1739 work was begun on the Mansion House. The

The Grocers' Hall in 1696; it was occupied by the Bank of England from 1695 to 1734.

Lord Mayor was at last to have an official residence worthy of his position. Building was finished in 1753 and, with the Bank of England and the Royal Exchange already there, the Bank crossroads began to take on something of its present appearance.

The change in this area produced a change in another. The old Stocks Market had to move out to make way for the Mansion House; it took over the area of what is now Ludgate Circus and established itself as the Fleet Market. The area was paved and roofed over and had shops instead of stalls; to the Londoners of the time this was an entirely new conception of a market.

Good paving in Fleet Market then, but it was some time later, and out of our period, before strict enough regulations brought about an improvement in the paving and general condition of the City streets themselves. One innovation of the time should be noted, however (as indeed it was noted and commented favourably on by visitors to London)—the installation in the 1740s of five thousand glass lanterns to provide the City with all-night lighting, which made it perhaps the best-lit urban area anywhere in the world. It is tempting to suggest that it was also partly out of a desire to display its superior brilliance to the upstart new areas that the City finally demolished its walls in 1762.

Georgian London was a London grown and still growing, gracefully in the West, haphazardly in the East, internationally in the City. Some areas were rural in character, others were densely populated and semi-industrialised.

Life in Georgian London

London was a city of contrasts, then, and with an entertainment value second to none. 'The man who is tired of London is tired of life,' said Dr Johnson, and while it remains true of 'something-for-everyone' London today, there is little doubt that then the attractions were offered with more gusto and excitement than in the more sophisticated and self-conscious 20th century. For spontaneity and lack of self-consciousness was the basis of the Georgian character, both high and low. The frank speech and forthright approach of the 'gentleman' differed little from that of the Thames waterman; the difference showed in dress and gesture, not in outlook. Squire Western in *Tom Jones* (vividly portrayed by Hugh Griffith in the recent film), though of the gentry rather than the aristocracy, exemplifies the Georgian character. Even when overlaid with 'the genteel behaviour and polite manner', the below-the-surface personality retained the below-the-stairs attitude to morals. While the upper classes continued to wench and curse there was little chance that the Society for the Reformation of

Manners would have much success with their tract, 'Kind Cautions Against Swearing', handed out to London hackney coachmen.

No, the difference showed in dress and manner, so before embarking on a look at various aspects of London life, it would be well to stop and get a picture of what Londoners looked like.

Dress

The design of clothes reveals the same sense of order which dominated all the arts of the Georgian period. And indeed it was probably at this time that the tailor emerged as an artist in his own right and became a designer conscious of the importance of all the elements—colour, pattern, material—blending into a whole.

This of course applies to the apparel of the lady and the gentleman; elegance was not for the poor. Their clothes remained cheap and functional. The cheapness and availability of cotton later in the period had a tremendous effect on cleanliness and hygiene among the poor, the necessity of washing their clothes inspiring the habit of washing themselves. Until then the 'great unwashed' wore rough clothes, which were seldom if ever changed. Women, for example, lived and slept in their leather full-boned stays—'never washed although worn day by day for years'. The washing woman in her leather stays was a familiar London street sight. When something was worn on top of them it was generally a separate jacket and skirt.

Among the upper classes, in the fashionable world of the *beau monde,* the costume for members of both sexes became more elaborate and colourful as the period progresses. For the ladies, Queen Mary had set the fashion for chintz and printed calicos. The basic garment for women was the open robe, a gown, combining bodice

Ladies and gentlemen of fashion in the reign of George I.

and skirt, the skirt opening at the front to reveal the petticoat. The bustle was in fashion until 1710, then it was replaced by the hoop, which came in various shapes and sizes—the bell, the fan (1740–50) and the oblong (1740–60). In George II's reign, skirts were befrilled and sported panniers on either side. Out-of-doors hooded cloaks over the head and clogs or pattens (leather or velvet stitched with gold braid) on the feet were worn. Generally shoes had massive heels, pointed toes and huge, square tongues.

Before turning to men's fashions, we should take a look in the lady's mirror as she prepared to dress herself in these clothes.

The Toilet (and also the lack of it)

Dressing was only half of the daily ceremony; making up was the other. The fashionable London lady of George II's time used strong perfumes—perhaps just as well, since not only the poor were members of the 'great unwashed'. Hygiene, personal and otherwise, was notable for its absence in Georgian times. Table manners, for example, left much to be desired and much to be cleared up. A book on etiquette advised that it was better manners to wipe one's knife on one's napkin than on the bread or the table cloth. The elegant mansion was lucky if it had a lavatory; the elegant person was lucky if he or she didn't have B.O.

But let us join the lady as she prepared to cover this and other deficiencies. She has summoned her hand maidens, she has seated herself at her 'toiletta' (dressing table).

> 'And now, unveil'd, the toilet stands displayed
> Each silver vase in mystic order laid,
> First, robed in white, the nymph intent adores,
> With head uncover'd, the cosmetic powers.'

Pope thus describes the 'secret rites of pride' (in the *Rape of the Lock*) performed by the lady of fashion.

The time for 'awful beauty to put on all its arms'—the puffs, powders, patches—took at a conservative estimate two hours. Obviously the amount of time depended on the amount of improvement or repair work to be done; 'plaistering up her ruins' was as much the business of cosmetics as the delicate heightening of natural beauty. The lady of fashion, beautiful though she may have been, dared not appear in polite society without powder and paint. 'Having left red and white quite off' she was liable to be described as 'one of the coarsest brown women'.

Unfortunately from the preservation point of view the 'white paint' they used had much the same effect on the skin as the household white paint of today would have. A basic component was white lead; this tended to ruin the skin, not to mention the stomach, and tended to make the hair come out in sympathy. It is said they frequently got the shakes and it was not unknown for death to be the final outcome of the treatment—'a victim to cosmetics' was the phrase used at the time. The sad thing is that the ladies were either not aware or refused to believe that cosmetics were the cause of the ravaging. Sometimes the ravaging had in fact been produced by other causes—by smallpox, for example, which was extremely prevalent at the time. This left in its wake nasty hollows in the skin—hollows which were ugly and had therefore to be disguised—that is, filled in by coarse white paint containing arsenic. A vicious circle. A few pox marks, spots or pimples could easily be concealed by the use of patches which remained fashionable till almost the end of the century; but more than a few spots necessitated more than a few black patches and the result must have been far from attractive. As a result 'beauty manufacturers' from the same breed of helpful murderers who sold the paints and powders advertised countless ointments and wonder cures for the damage which by and large they had caused in the first place.

On top of all this 'care' of the complexion there was the hair to be attended to. At the beginning of the period, this was a comparatively simple operation. The hair was closely dressed with a small top-knot decorated with little ornaments of lace or ribbon and covered with a dainty little cap fixed under the chin. But this simplicity was not to last and by the end of our period *haute coiffure* began to climb ever upwards to even greater extremes, until in the 70s and 80s the height of the hair almost equalled the height of the body.

Men's Fashion

If this seems extravagant, it must be remembered that women were being faced with great opposition from the men in matters of dress. Indeed, it was in the design of men's clothes that the tailor had a field day—if that doesn't suggest too much exertion. Most of the elegant gentlemen's clothes were designed for static pursuits, for sitting, standing and posing rather than moving about.

The major change was from the long tunic into the coat, which was waisted and had wide skirts stiffened with whalebone to make them stand out. The sleeves were short, wide and cuffed to show the shirt below. The coat was also cut short to reveal the tops of the stockings, rolled loosely over the breeches above the knee and high enough to join the bottom of the long, straight waistcoat or vest.

This was the basic design on which fashion rang the changes. For example, later, in George II's reign, the coat became even more tightly waisted and the skirts wider. The back became slit up the centre and the material buttoned back, and the front was left open to display more fully the flowered waistcoat beneath. For outdoor wear, either a surtout, a loose great-coat with a cape-like collar, or a cloak was worn. Shoes were high-heeled and high-tongued with square metal buckles (small till 1730). The toes were square (like the heels), until about 1740 when a rounder shape came in.

George II's reign became an era of self-expression as well as of good design, men wearing what they felt best suited their personalities. The great extrovert of the day was the beau—a colourful figure in an elaborately laced coat of silk, satin or velvet, manipulating a cane, an eye-glass and a snuffbox (and in winter, a muff) while at the same time carrying his tricorne hat for fear it would disarrange his curled wig.

By this time all sorts of wigs were in vogue—the Bag, the Ramillies, the Staircase, the Cauliflower, to mention a few. The high curled wig with the full bottom was the fashion until about 1720, when the Tye wig came in. This, with the hair drawn back and tied in the nape of the neck, was to remain the basic style, though many variations were performed on it, of which the most popular was probably the pigtail. For formal gatherings the wig was powdered and 'perfumed'; for informal occasions at home it was replaced by the night-cap or turban.

The gentleman's morning, like the lady's, was therefore taken up with the toilet, not at the 'toiletta' but at the shaving table. This might perhaps be one of Chippendale's with 'a folding Top, and a Glass to rise out with a Spring-Catch' and with 'Places for holding Soap, and other Necessaries', and behind them 'Places for Razors' and 'Places for Bottles'. While wigs were in fashion, men were clean-shaven and close-cropped, although occasionally they wore their own hair and powdered that—perhaps a necessary temporary measure after 'losing' their wigs in the London streets. John Gay in his *Trivia* describes how a small child, carried in a butcher's tray on one's shoulder, would lift wigs off passing strangers. Wig stealing was common, not only because wigs fetched good prices, but, as the steady trade in second-hand wigs showed, because they were worn not only by the rich or even the middling sort but by all. The bag-wig, for example, was worn first by servants to protect their hair while working. A foreign visitor in 1748 was astounded to find that 'farm servants, clodhoppers, day labourers . . . all labouring folk' were bewigged. These wigs were probably woollen since human hair cost 17s. 6d. a pound. But though wig-wearing and wig-making were widespread throughout the country, London remained the centre of high-class manufacture and, of course, of fashion.

Entertainments

Once into their finery, the upper classes up in London for the season would sally forth in sedan chair or coach from their West End mansion to the coffee houses or club, or to fulfil a social engagement with other members of the 'ton' (as the fashionable *beau monde* was called). This might be no more than a dinner party—though after a typical Georgian dinner, no more is what most people would be capable of—or it might be a visit to the theatre or the opera, or it might be a visit to Ranelagh.

Ranelagh was one of Georgian London's many pleasure gardens. It has been estimated that there were between 60 and 70 of these, though not all were successful and some were little more than taverns with gardens in the back. Certainly there was none to compare with Ranelagh, 'one of those public places of pleasure which is not to be equalled in Europe, and is the resort of people of the first quality'. Or, as Horace Walpole succinctly put it, where 'you can't set your foot without treading on a Prince or Duke of Cumberland'. In fact, the gardens themselves, beautiful though they were said to be, were less of an attraction than the rotunda, which had an internal diameter of 150 feet. In the centre of this, there was originally a huge four-sided arched structure, built to hold the orchestra; it was later turned into a central

A Hogarth drawing of the stage of the Drury Lane Theatre. Note that spectators are no longer seated on the stage.

fireplace and the orchestra filled up the place of one of the entrances. 'The entertainment consists of a band of music with an organ, accompanied by the best voices. The regale is tea and coffee.' This refreshment was served at long tables near the central fire or in recesses round the sides. But the main attraction of Ranelagh was neither the refreshment nor the music, good as it was. (In 1764, the eight-year-old Mozart gave a concert of his own compositions.) It was simply the desire to be seen there, as it is at a film première or first night in the theatre today. But the company was not so much first-nighters as every-nighters. Horace Walpole wrote, 'every night constantly I go to Ranelagh, which can totally beat Vauxhall.'

Vauxhall was another favourite pleasure garden; it was, in fact, the oldest. It spread over about twelve acres on the south side of the river just opposite Westminster Abbey. (Ranelagh was further upriver, on the north bank, to the south-east of the Royal Hospital at Chelsea.) Originally Spring Gardens at the time of the Restoration, Vauxhall really came into its own after 1730 when it was enlarged and improved. Again there was a rotunda, where indoor musical entertainment was provided. There was also music in the gardens themselves with their fine walks and triumphal arches. Here you could hear the music but you couldn't see the band, who were concealed in a hole in the ground behind a clump of 'musical' bushes, as they were called by the proprietor. What the band in the pit called them has unfortunately not come down to us, but at all events the experiment didn't last long; it must have been an early example of 'rain stopped play'.

Vauxhall was less exclusive than Ranelagh; indeed, it was open to all. Rich and poor, the *beau monde* and the underworld all rubbed shoulders, and if in the process of rubbing, a valuable watch or snuffbox changed hands, that was all in the game. In the game too, or rather on it, were many of the young ladies who attended. A foreign visitor was astounded by 'the boldness of the women of the town, who in the most shameless manner importuned'. This would have been less shocking to the regulars, even the fashionable set, among whom it was the custom to frequent the better sort of bawdy house, like Mrs. Cole's in Covent Garden. For those who preferred messing about on the river there was The Folly—a floating bawdy-house and tavern anchored in the middle of the Thames just opposite Somerset House.

Other outdoor sports were indulged in by the rich. On the country estates there was of course hunting, shooting and fishing—hunting for any kind of animal which could be pursued, a list which included that attractive

An early game of cricket (1743), as played on the Artillery Ground. Note the scorer notching up the runs.

two-legged animal, the female servant. But in town there was also the newly adopted 'in' sport—cricket. This caught on as an upper-class pursuit in London. In Queen Anne's day the most famous of the many cricket clubs which sprang up was the Artillery Ground, Finsbury, where the Honourable Artillery Club still play today. In 1744 a Kent versus All England match was played—the first game of which we have a record of the score. Some forty years later, just after the end of our period, Thomas Lord's first cricketground was opened, though not on the present site of Lord's. To begin with, cricket had few, if any, rules; by the match of 1744 some rules were fixed, including 'ye pitching of ye first Wicket is to be determined by ye Cast of a piece of money'. Also there were to be four balls to an over. The Batsmen or striker was warned 'if he runs out of his Ground to hinder a catch, it's Out', but was also advised that if 'he nips a Ball up just before him, he may fall before his Wicket . . . to save it.' Not so much Leg-before-wicket as Body-before-wicket. Umpires were cautioned 'to mark the Ball that it may not be changed' and also to clamp down on 'frivolous delays'—an intriguing phrase which suggests that brighter cricket was no problem at the time.

But if the game was played with gusto and occasional frivolity it had its serious side for heavy bets were laid on the result. This is not unexpected in an age where gambling, always a great English pastime—some would call it a disease—was possibly indulged in more than at any other period. Gambling at the racetrack, betting on cockfights, speculating on the Stock Market were all indulged in by both rich and poor.

At the race track 'the vast company . . . contains all mankind on equal footing from the Duke to the country peasant'. Most race meetings were small local affairs, the only national meeting being at Newmarket, where horse and jockey battled to win plates presented by Queen Anne, a keen follower of the horses—so keen in fact that the money for the plates came out of the secret service funds. The sleek racehorse of today had not yet evolved then, but it was about this time that breeders began to introduce the Arab and Barbary blood which eventually brought about the change.

In London much the same sort of 'vast company of all classes' gathered at cockfights, a favourite national sport, at which a foreigner 'would certainly conclude the assembly to be all mad, by their continual outcries of Six to Four, Five to One, repeated with great earnestness, every Spectator taking part with his favourite cock, as if it were a party cause'.

Cockfighting, and more especially horse-racing, could be enjoyed by all classes. So, too, sad to say, were executions. Public hangings were of course not new, but the opportunity to watch them increased during the 18th century as the number of capital offences rose from 50 to 250. Well might Henry Fielding write of the executions at Tyburn: 'We sacrifice the lives of men, not for the reformation but for the diversion of the populace.' But his was a voice in the wilderness; the more common point of view was expressed by Dr Johnson: 'Sir, executions are intended to draw spectators. If they do not draw spectators they don't answer their purpose.' The fact that their purpose, presumably to act as a deterrent, was far from being achieved will be considered elsewhere. For the present it is enough to record that hangings were enjoyed by all classes, from the London journeyman who took a day off every six weeks to watch them, to the members of the *beau monde*, who would meet for breakfast together, before going off to Tyburn. And after the hanging they would no doubt retire to their favourite coffee house to talk about it.

Coffee Houses

'These houses are extremely convenient. You have all

Manner of News there: you have a good Fire which you may sit by as long as you please: you have a Dish of Coffee, you meet your friends for the Transaction of Business, and all for a Penny, if you don't care to spend more.'

'These houses' were of course the coffee houses for which the 18th century is famed. The first had been opened as early as 1656, and despite the complaints of neighbours unaccustomed to the 'evill smells' of coffee, the habit soon caught on. By the reign of Queen Anne there were some 500 in London. Macaulay wrote: 'the coffee-house was the Londoner's home, and . . . those who wished to find a gentleman commonly asked, not whether he lived in Fleet Street or Chancery Lane, but whether he frequented the Grecian or the Rainbow.'

People of similar interests tended to congregate at a favourite coffee house, to exchange news and views, to exercise their freedom of speech and almost incidentally to drink coffee. It was a regular daily (if not twice or thrice daily) habit. At first, the principal value of the coffee house was as a primitive communications centre. 'Hawking about for news' was a necessary occupation at a time when business was booming and newspapers were scarce. The coffee house, though it attracted the gossip, catered more for the hard news-seeking businessman, whose stocks and shares could be affected by accidents of nature or the wars of man. The role of the coffee house in business is best illustrated by the fact that the Stock Exchange virtually grew out of Garraway's and Jonathan's in Change Alley. Similarly Lloyd's, the great marine insurance agency and centre of shipping intelligence, whose home is now an enormous building in Leadenhall Street, was once simply the name of a coffee house. Edward Lloyd used to post up shipping news for his clients, which did not then appear in the newspapers. Eventually, he brought out the first *Lloyd's News*, which lasted only nine months, and then, in 1734, *Lloyd's List*, which has lasted to this day and shows no signs of fading away.

The need for accurate information led to the growth of the newspaper industry. The first newspaper was published in 1622, entitled *The Certain News of the Present Week*, but before the reign of Queen Anne, apart from many news-sheets dealing with politics rather than general events, there were few newspapers in the ordinary sense. *The London Gazette* had been coming out thrice weekly since 1668; in the early years of the 18th century it was joined by several others, notably the *London Post* and *A Review of the English Nation*, edited by Daniel Defoe. The first daily paper—unless you count *The Post-Boy*, which died after three days in 1695—was *The Daily Courant*, which appeared in 1702. The first newspapers had a small circulation. Apart from a three-halfpenny library in the Strand, where you could go and read them, the best place to get hold of them was the coffee house. And with the development of the newspaper, the printed word slowly took over from the spoken word. Business became less informal, but relics of the way it used to be conducted survive today, such as the motto of the Stock Exchange, 'a man's word is his bond', and the persistence of verbal transactions, and serve as reminders of its coffee-house origins.

'Coffee-house talk' turned to the printed word in another way. Particular coffee houses, such as Will's near Covent Garden, were the meeting places of literary men like Addison, Steele, Swift and Johnson. And while they were meeting there, other groups assembled in other chosen coffee houses brought together by a shared interest or outlook—Whigs at St. James's, Tories at the Cocoa Tree, the clergy at Truby's, to name a few. Virtually all coteries were catered for. They were not exclusive, but the tendency to exclusion was there, and the half-open door was firmly shut as the coffee house evolved into the club.

The Clubs

Generally speaking the formation of the club was perhaps inevitable in such a class-conscious society with its minute but clear-cut gradations. Even so, it would be a mistake to think of the club only in terms of the upper classes, like today's image of a club full of upper-crusty old military gentlemen, outdated clergymen and politicians of shared social standing, with a kind of hush brooding over their closed world. Aristocratic clubs there certainly were, but there was little hush. Group talk was still a major attraction; among others were, needless to say, eating and drinking, and, equally predictably, gambling. Clubs like White's, the chief Tory haunt (significantly perhaps, the first coffee house to become a club in 1693) and later Boodle's and Brook's, the club for the Whigs (all still to be found in St. James's Street) were the gambling centres of the fashionable world.

But not all the clubs were for the aristocracy. The 'clubable' man (to use Dr Johnson's word) was the one who felt the need for companionship of his own kind, and since it takes all kinds, there were all kinds of clubs. The Mitre Club in Essex Street, founded by Johnson for the literary-minded, was perhaps inevitable, but the Humdrum Club where members met for the purpose of saying nothing was less predictable. There was (though not surprisingly in London) a Club of Fat Men, big in size if not in membership (members 15, collective weight three tons) whose qualification for entry was an inability to pass through the door; another wider entrance was unfolded to admit the successful candidate once he'd been dislodged from the first. Those wishing to join that club should perhaps have gone on a training course at the Beef Steak Club (which still survives) or perhaps the Kit Kat Club, named after Christopher Kat a manufacturer of mutton pies, though the avowed purpose of this club (founded by supporters of the Hanoverian Succession) was unrestricted evening conversation. Certainly with Congreve, Steele, Addison and Vanbrugh among its forty or so members, there should have been no lack of topics to discuss.

The number of these new fraternities is limitless. Considerate students at Oxford founded the Amorous Club, where those in love could sigh and rave at each other without boring those not in a similar condition. Among the latter were possibly some members of the Ugly Club. Business-minded, money-mad Georgian society also had its dropouts—the Lazy Club. A member wrote: 'We generally come in night-gowns, without stockings above our heels, and sometimes but one on. Our salutation on entrance is a yawn and a stretch and then without more ceremony we take our places upon the lolling-table.' A communal sleep-in no less.

Drink

There is little doubt what the Georgians' favourite pastime was, however. More even than gambling, they loved to drink. 'Drunk as a lord'—the phrase is an 18th-century invention, and it speaks for itself. Drunkenness was universal through all classes but the lead came from the top. Even political meetings were arranged so as not to clash with drinking habits. Wine, brandy, punch and rum were the favourites but much 'lemonade' was also drunk—not surprisingly, since the recipe was equal parts brandy, white wine and water, with half a lemon. 'Dead drunk' was often a literal description (notably among the poor, where, as we shall see, gin wrought a terrible toll) and many more 'hastened [their] end by an over-indulgence in strong liquors'. Women as well as men drank to excess. Liquor was cheap and plentiful. At home the sideboard was well-stocked (not to mention the wine cellar) for the constant stream of visitors. When they didn't visit you, you visited them and used up their supply. If the social engagement took the form of an outing, there were few places you could go to and not be surrounded by drink.

The Poor

We left the upper-classes, appropriately enough, in their cups but it is equally apposite to begin our consideration of the life of the poorer people with the same topic—drink.

To the poor who scratched a bare existence among filthy streets and ramshackle homes drink was not part of an ebullient round of social engagements; it was a means of escape from the intolerable circumstances in which they lived. Beer was the staple tipple, drunk like, and instead of, water. Benjamin Franklin (the great American statesman who spent 18 months in London as a printer in the 1720's) wrote of his pot-boy: 'My companion at press drank every day a pint before breakfast, a pint at breakfast, a pint between breakfast and dinner, a pint in the afternoon about 6 o'clock, and another pint when he had done his day's work.' Franklin was that rare thing, a water drinker, but even he had to pay his contribution to the drink funds of the printing house. These funds, generally raised from new apprentices (among shipwrights, the penalty for defaulting was flogging with a hand saw) were further added to by a system of fines. Franklin says of his pot-boy: 'It was necessary he supposed to drink strong beer that he might be strong to labour.'

But if excessive drinking was common to all trades it was difficult for it to be otherwise. The public house was the centre of the tradesman's working life. He got his wages there on Saturday; it acted as an employment exchange if he was out of work. 'The house of call,' as it was known, 'is an ale house where they [the tradesmen] generally use, the landlord knows where to find them, and masters go there to enquire when they want hands.'

'Macaronis', as young bucks of the town were called, drinking asses' milk sold in the street.

Outside working hours there was equally little chance of getting away from drink. 'All the amusements of the working people of the metropolis were immediately connected with drinking,' wrote Francis Place, himself a former tradesman, 'chair clubs, chanting clubs, lottery clubs, and every variety of club, intended for amusement, were always held at public houses.'

Drunkenness could lead to disorder, disorder to prison, but even here there was no escape from drink. Many of the smaller prisons were *in* public houses, and in the larger ones the keeper was allowed to sell beer for his own profit. Moreover, the constable in the parish watch-house was frequently a publican who turned the watch-house into a pub. How you were treated overnight, while waiting to come up before the justice in the morning, depended on how much you spent on drink.

We have seen something of the state in which the poor lived. It is tempting to dwell at length on these horrifying conditions but the situation, though worsened, was not new to the London of the period. It is more profitable, therefore, to concentrate on how, towards the end of the period, something at last began to be done to alleviate the situation.

We have just outlined the near impossibility of avoiding drink and drunkenness, but drunk on beer is one thing, and drunk on spirits is another. It was the spread of gin-drinking that was to reduce London's poor to the lowest depths of degradation. Between the 1720s and 1750s gin (or geneva) drinking wrought a terrible havoc. There were more burials than baptisms. Gin killed off the adult, reduced the birthrate and weakened the children who were born; the annual loss in population caused by the shrinking birthrate, and premature death of children under five was assessed at over 9000 between 1740 and 1750. Despite the obvious results of this gin orgy, little was done for the simple reason that spirit drinking was encouraged. The distilling industry was 'one of the most essential things to support the landed interest . . . and therefore especially to be preserved and tenderly used' wrote Defoe (although to be fair, before the orgy was really under way). With such an attitude prevalent, however, it is hardly surprising that occasional attempts to remedy the situation failed, and that 'strip-me-naked', as the gin was called, was allowed to take its toll. No licence was needed to sell it and it was estimated that an average of one house in four was a gin shop.

The effects on a population living at a bare subsistence level can be imagined. What started off as a cheap means of escape ended up as a craving which had to be satisfied. M. Dorothy George (author of *London Life in the Eighteenth Century,* perhaps the best documented account of the life and work of the poor at this period) quotes the case of a girl who removed her child from a workhouse so that she could strangle it and sell its clothes for money to buy gin. Clearly Hogarth's horrifying *Gin Lane* was no caricature. This picture had a powerful effect on the public conscience and formed part of a general campaign mounted in 1751. An Act of that year, forced on Parliament by the campaign, had an immediate effect on reducing the sale of gin.

The effect of gin on the London 'mob' and on crimes of violence should have been clear. Perhaps because drunkenness was not considered a vice or because it was a habit of all classes, the obvious connection between gin and violence seemed less obvious then. The increase in crime was noted of course, but the only steps taken to halt it were those to the gallows. The number of capital offences was raised in a misguided and vain attempt to lower the number of crimes. Significantly, perhaps, in a society run by the moneyed classes—a society in which one of the main causes of the increased crime rate was attributed by foreigners to the great gap between the rich and poor, who nonetheless rubbed shoulders in the London streets—the majority of the new crimes

The branding of a criminal, one of the penalties for non-capital offences. Brutal punishments led to more crime not less in the 18th century.

punishable by death were for crimes committed against property. Attempted murder went lightly punished; but pick a pocket, and if what you stole was worth more than a shilling, you were off on the two-hour cart journey from Newgate Prison to Tyburn, seated on your own coffin, jeered and cheered at by the throngs on the way.

For 'lesser' crimes, the penalty was whipping and branding, again in full view of the public, or being put in the pillory or stocks, when the crowd could join in the punishing by pelting the prisoner with mud and stones. The deterrent principle behind this is questionable; it would seem more likely to encourage the spread of violence and crime. In fact, the number of hangings increased as the century progressed.

The Reformers

What was really required to combat the crime wave was, of course, a good police force. This was not to come into existence until the following century, but in the 1750s London's first 'policemen' might be said to have been 'Mr. Fielding's people'. Henry Fielding, the creator of *Tom Jones*, should equally be remembered from his work as a magistrate, probably the first uncorruptible holder of this office in London. From his office in Bow Street, Fielding, his brother John (later Sir John) and Saunders Welsh waged war against the crime and corruption of the day. Their first step was to undermine one of the main methods of arrest, the system of the 'thief-taker'—a man who was paid by the number of criminals he caught. When both thief-taker and magistrate rely for their remuneration on the number and severity of the crimes brought to justice, the danger of corruption is obvious. Fielding sought to eliminate this system by advertising in the press for the public to report crimes committed against them to his office, with descriptions of their loss and of the criminal when possible. This was a

A public whipping in the London Sessions House Yard. Such punishments were usually carried out outside the prisons.

novel idea at the time, but once people realised that Fielding was genuinely trying to help them (his humane treatment of cases in court helped to persuade them) they responded. In addition, Fielding established his 'people', a miniature police force whose role was similar to the thief-taker except that the men were highly trained and carefully picked for their resistence to bribery and corruption.

His brother John, the Blind Beak, carried on the work alone after Henry's death. 'Alone' is the operative word, for other magistrates were slow to follow the Bow Street example. John Fielding's efforts at reform extended beyond the immediate influence of his court. He became associated with Jonas Hanway in his philanthropic work among poor children, victims of the inadequate Poor Laws and the parish apprenticeship system. To aid the boys, ill-treated and as a result, frequently delinquent, Fielding, Hanway and others set up the Marine Society, which aimed to equip boys for training as officers' servants. To help orphaned girls and reformed prostitutes, Fielding and Hanway founded the Magdalen Hospital.

Hanway, appalled by the fact that 'few parish apprentices lived to be apprenticed', turned his attention to the plight of infants, but it took many years of persistence before Parliament passed an Act in 1769 compelling London parishes to send their parish infants to be nursed in the country.

Infant welfare was also the concern of Captain Thomas Coram. The foundling, left deserted on the doorstep, or more simply in the street, was as great a contributor to the infant death-rate as the child of the gin addict or the baby killed by smallpox. Captain Coram campaigned for 17 years before his project for a Founding Hospital was fulfilled by the granting of a charter. Built by private subscription, and aided by art exhibitions (to which Hogarth contributed) and performances

A grisly invitation to the execution of Jonathan Wild.

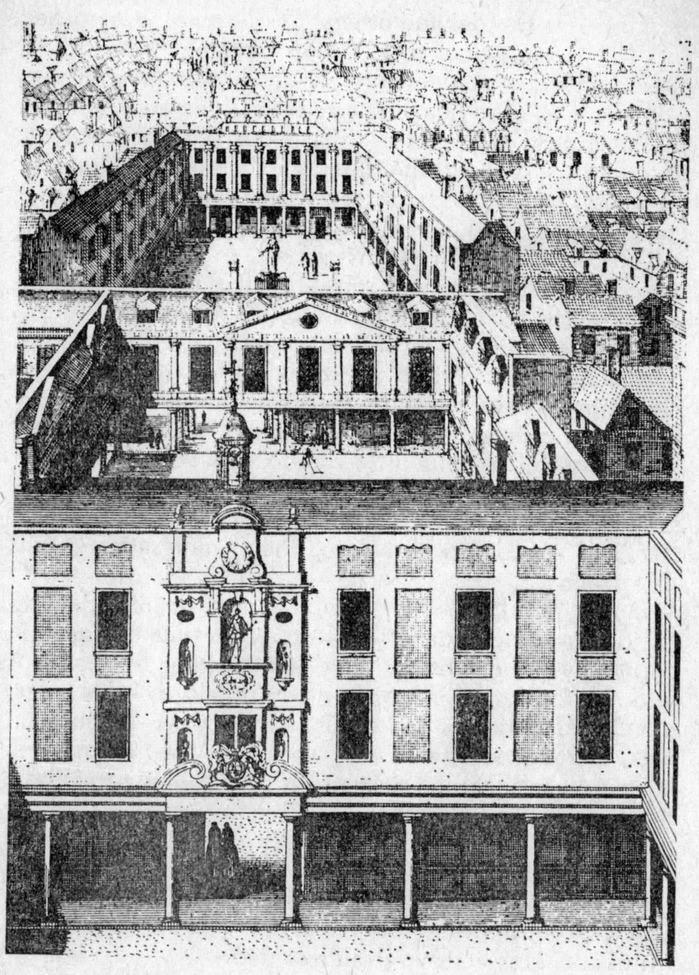

St. Thomas's Hospital, rebuilt in the reign of Anne. St. Thomas's, together with several newly built hospitals, contributed to an improvement in health and hygiene in the mid-century.

of music (by Handel and others), the hospital was opened in 1745 on the site of what is now Coram's Fields.

Unhappily, overconfidence in the hospital's ability to save the lives of so many children led to the donation of a parliamentary grant, on the disastrous condition that all foundlings taken to the hospital should be admitted. Needless to say, thousands of children were brought to it from all over London, and the resulting congestion undermined the whole aim of saving lives. In 1760 Parliament remedied its mistake and sensibly left the hospital to be run as a private charity with controlled admission.

The growing body of philanthropists spread their work over many fields. Prison reform was the aim of General Oglethorpe. The corruption and cruelty of warders in the Fleet and Marshalsea debtors' prisons was investigated at his instigation, but little reform was achieved at the time. Oglethorpe sought to alleviate the lot of the debtor and the poor in general by the founding of Georgia in the New World and by helping their immigration to this new colony.

By the middle of the century a quite definite drop in the death-rate crowned the efforts of the philanthropist in improving the conditions in which the poor lived. But it also marked an improvement in medical knowledge, which led to a greater chance of survival. Inoculation was introduced (from Turkey) and the Inoculation Hospital had some success in controlling smallpox. Scottish doctors, the Hunters, William Smellie and Sir John Pringle, brought their superior skills to London, causing revolutionary changes in surgery, midwifery and hygiene. Hospitals sprang up. Between 1720 and 1745, Guy's, Westminster, St. George's, the London and Middlesex Hospitals were all founded.

It is typical of the period, and a part-explanation of why the age of reform was so slow to get under way, that hospitals like these were created not out of municipal concern for the community welfare but out of the efforts

Above: *'Gin Lane', Hogarth's famous portrayal of the misery and deg*
tion caused by drink among the London poor.

Right: *Church Row, Hampstead, a particularly fine example of a gra*
Georgian terrace.

Previous page: *A detail of a capital at St. Alphege, Greenwich* (1712).
church was designed by Nicholas Hawksmoor, who succeeded Wren a
chief architect of London's churches.

Above: *The west front of St. Paul's Cathedral. Wren's great undertak begun in 1675, was finally completed in 1711.*

Right: *The façade of Morden College, Blackheath, designed by Wren Sir John Morden, a City merchant, in 1695.*

Above: *A detail of a typical early 18th-century doorway. Note the f light and the lampstand in the foreground.*

Right: *The Manor House, Croom's Hill, Greenwich, built in 1697.*

The statue of Sir Joshua Reynolds in the forecourt of the Royal Acade
of Arts (founded in 1768), of which he was the first president.

of individuals or small groups banded together in common humanity.

The question why the 'establishment' was not concerned is, perhaps, best answered by quoting the theory of Soame Jenyns 'that the sufferings of individuals are absolutely necessary to universal happiness'. It was part of the general ordering of the universe which presupposed that 'whatever is, is right'. So if there was poverty it was right that there was, and it was surely none of the business of those who were given wealth to interfere with things as they were. This sort of self-satisfied distortion of the scientific outlook, which allowed the rich to rest complacently on their morals (themselves in need of reform) was the outlook the new philanthropy had to attack and conquer before the conscience of the nation as a whole could be stirred. In the meantime, philanthropy and medicine did what they could for the social and physical needs of the poor. Nor were their minds and souls left uncared for. As far back as Anne's reign the foundation of the Charity Schools had taken the education of the poor in hand, in the hope that being able to read would lead them to a devoted study of the Bible and to a more virtuous life. They can hardly be said to have achieved that aim, but any education was better than none. Later, in the 1740s, the Evangelical movement got under way. This was a revival of 'old time religion', preached with enthusiasm and warmth, the qualities most lacking in (and in fact despised by) the Augustan Christian, whose cool outlook was inspired by the 'reasonableness of Christianity', to use Locke's phrase.

John Wesley is, of course, the most famous of the new breed of Evangelists, the Billy Graham of his day. It is typical of the Augustan outlook that the preservation of the *status quo* was preferred to the successful conversion of thousands, so that Methodism was forced to break from the established church. This was the last thing wished for by Wesley. Methodism had started out simply as a religious society in Oxford formed by John and Charles Wesley, William Law and George Whitefield to restore greater discipline (that is, method) to worship. Their Evangelism was not intended to bring about a new church.

The forces of reform were accumulating, and of them the Evangelical movement was to prove the strongest—strong enough, in fact, to transform Georgian life altogether. By the end of our period, middle-class morality was already on the march.

The Age of Grace

The 18th century has been called by John Gloag the 'Golden Age of good design, wherein hardly anything was made without the impress of good taste, allied with superbly competent craftsmanship and, most important of all, lucid common sense'. The period may have been full of smells offensive to the modern nose, but there was little, if anything, to offend the eye. The key word to the age is grace; and if it reaches its fullest bloom on 'the long flat plain of the Hanoverian Age' the buds can already be seen from the Revolution onwards. Good taste, style, elegance, harmony, these inform the design of almost everything from the stately mansion down to the confectioner's label.

The Georgian aristocracy may have been constantly in their cups, but the cups themselves were always of superb design. In fact, the picture of a boisterous drunk at an elegantly designed table, beautiful glass in hand, could stand as a useful shorthand image of the period. This uniform good taste in design stems from architecture, and it is therefore architecture we must first consider before looking at anything else.

Architecture

Perhaps the most basic influence on the new manner of building was the rise of the individual architect. Previously buildings had been planned by corporate bodies such as the Church or the town council; the work may have been in the hands of an individual, but an anonymous one (at least to us) working within, and no doubt directed by, that body. In the previous century, the architect began to emerge as an independent figure, perhaps appointed by the crown, but with a much greater degree of freedom than before. Men like Inigo Jones and Christopher Wren (who each held the post of Surveyor General to the crown) were the forerunners of the countless free-lance architects of the post-Revolution period. The rise of the profession revolutionised architecture. There was less emphasis on craftsmanship and materials as such and much more on the intellectual approach to the building to be planned.

Inigo Jones studied in Italy for some years. The ideas he absorbed there were to have far-reaching implications. The influence of Italy on the architecture of the 'classical' era is profound; England was virtually given an Italian facelift. The new buildings were so un-English in appearance and character that a hostile reaction towards what might seem the whim of a few architects might have been expected. The reverse is nearer the truth. The new 'classical' buildings were exactly to the taste and mood of the Georgian age. The aftermath of the Revolution with its elimination of the theory of the Divine Right of Kings and its raising of the status of Parliament to the equivalent of the Roman Senate, the rapidly expanding empire, which 'carried our arms and victories beyond where Roman eagles ever flew', the innate 'classicism' of the age—(that is, the sense of permanence, of 'having arrived')—all created a kinship and a friendly rivalry with ancient Roman civilisation. Admiration led to emulation

A lady in a sedan chair (with a boisterous companion) crossing Covent Garden in 1747. Covent Garden had been a fruit and vegetable market since 1671.

The Grand Tour, that 'finishing school' of the young aristocracy, offered a first-hand view of Roman architecture and a closer acquaintance with the works of the Italian Renaissance architect Palladio. Hence the introduction of the Palladian style of building to England. (Hence, too, the later development of the extremist worship of the past. The love of ancient buildings deteriorated into a love of ruins in themselves to the extent of designing and building ruins.)

To build in 'the good Roman manner' therefore became the aim. The mentor was Andrea Palladio, who from a study of ancient buildings had drawn up a strict set of rules for classical proportions. These rules had been known in England since Tudor times, but the Elizabethan and Jacobean temperament was not suited to such severity. Also first-hand knowledge was lacking. The influence of Inigo Jones was not freely felt until after his lifetime; it largely affected the men who followed him, principally Christopher Wren. He rather than Jones succeeded in anglicising the Italian style, observing the classical rules but using English materials like brick.

But Wren was far from being a pure classicist. While his genius held sway Palladianism would have to wait. Wren, a man of many interests before he turned to architecture, became an architect who took ideas from many different sources. He borrowed styles from France and Holland as well as Rome, and it is a measure of his originality that he succeeded in welding these different parts into a whole inimitably his own. His work is usually labelled Baroque, but it is really only in the last stages of his career that this term can be applied to his buildings. St. Stephen, Walbrook, for example, one of his masterpieces, was 'yet serene enough to delight the Palladian Lord Burleigh'.

Wren is best known for his churches, but he nevertheless exercised great influence on the design of houses. The character of the town house of Queen Anne's reign

St. Mary-le-Bow (the home of Bow Bells), rebuilt by Wren after the Great Fire (and rebuilt again after the Blitz).

stems from his solution to the problem of adapting the classical style (best suited for mansions or palaces) to the needs of the averagely prosperous citizen. This 'Queen Anne' house showed Wren borrowing from Holland, where the style originated. The basic shape was rectangular and the basic impression of symmetry and proportion. To preserve this proportion, the top storey where necessary was put in the roof above the eaves, so that the horizontal line of the rectangle was retained. This device, the attic storey with dormer windows, is familiar enough to us now but was a novelty then, although Inigo Jones had first experimented with it. The Queen Anne house was built in stone or brick with projecting corner stones or blocks of bricks, placed in a long-short-by-short pattern. The same pattern framed the windows. But perhaps the most striking feature (at the time) was the actual window frames themselves, for it was at this time that the sash-window first slid on to the English scene and 'had almost as great an effect upon the character and proportions of houses as the use of the classic orders'.

Georgian Houses

The advantage of the sash-window as a harmonising agent can be seen as we move on to look at the town houses of the Georgian period. It became the only type of window used on town houses until half-way through the 19th century, and because of its usefulness as a unifying feature in the planning of built-up areas it is understandable why it was used so exclusively. London and other towns (notably Bath) were now embarking on an era of town-planning—a necessary step, for towns were by this time both overcrowded and still expanding at a brisk rate. The problem was not only how to house the many but also how to do so in a manner that would satisfy the demands of well-proportioned, symmetrical building. The solution was the terrace. The street, rather than the individual house, was to be the architectural unit. Eighteenth-century terraces were generally simple buildings, four storeys high, usually of brick, with the basic rectangular shape preserved by hiding the slope of the roofs behind stone-topped parapets. The chimney-stacks, regularly spaced, were placed on the thick dividing walls between the individual houses. (Their thickness was mainly a fire precaution.) The unifying sash-windows were beautifully proportioned: short windows on the ground floor giving a sense of solidity; tall windows on the first floor suggesting grandeur (the main rooms of the house were on the first floor); shorter again for the second floor; and square windows on the top to finish off the design. The house was reached by a short flight of steps to the panelled front door topped by a semi-circular fanlight.

Thus the terrace became the commonest type of housing for the advancing middle class. In the form of either straight streets, crescents or squares, the terrace changed the face of London. It was the standard town-planning device, and clearly its supremacy could never have been achieved if house building had been left to the individual householder, though in fact building was less in the hands of the corporate body than of the 'speculator'. This figure had emerged with the speedy rebuilding after the Great Fire of 1666. The device of the building lease —introduced by the Earl of Southampton, the developer of Bloomsbury—was seized upon by speculators as a method of getting rich quick. Landowners exploited their properties; those without land rushed to purchase and exploit it. The danger of 'jerry-building' was obvious, and indeed much of it was practiced. But by and large, the standard of building was high, and the planning admirable. Why should it be otherwise, when 'all men of education, up to the end of the Georgian period, could design a passable house'?

English Baroque

In the meantime the anglicised classicism of Wren had developed into Baroque, which, according to T. W. West was 'a Classical Renaissance architecture that developed in a highly original and often un-Classical way, sacrificing rules and convention in order to achieve arresting effects of grandeur and complexity, richness and movement'. In England this style is most closely associated with Nicholas Hawksmoor and Sir John Vanbrugh. Hawksmoor (1661–1776), a pupil of Wren, took over from the master the building of new churches. They are generally massive, bold in silhouette with 'imposing and dramatic' towers and theatrical in effect, appealing to the emotions rather than to cool intellectual appreciation.

But it is the work of Sir John Vanbrugh (1664–1726) which most fully expresses the Baroque movement in England. His huge country houses, designed to accommodate not so much the aristocracy as their collection of art treasures, were status symbols with a vengeance. Rules of proportion were sacrificed in order to produce a general effect of grandeur. In fact, effect was all to the Baroque architect. It didn't matter what you did or how exaggerated it was, as long as the effect was stunning. Vanbrugh when designing Blenheim Palace and Castle Howard relied mainly for his effect on sheer monumental size. Such ostentation, however, is alien to the English character and the Baroque movement gave way to a more sober style.

After the extravagance of Baroque, Palladianism was on the way in again. The time was now ripe for it. By the 1730s, the Augustan Age, a 'classical' age of conformity and good taste, was well under way and the set rules of Palladio were adopted as the standard of good architecture in a way that was impossible when Inigo Jones first introduced them.

Lord Burlington was the prime mover, but other

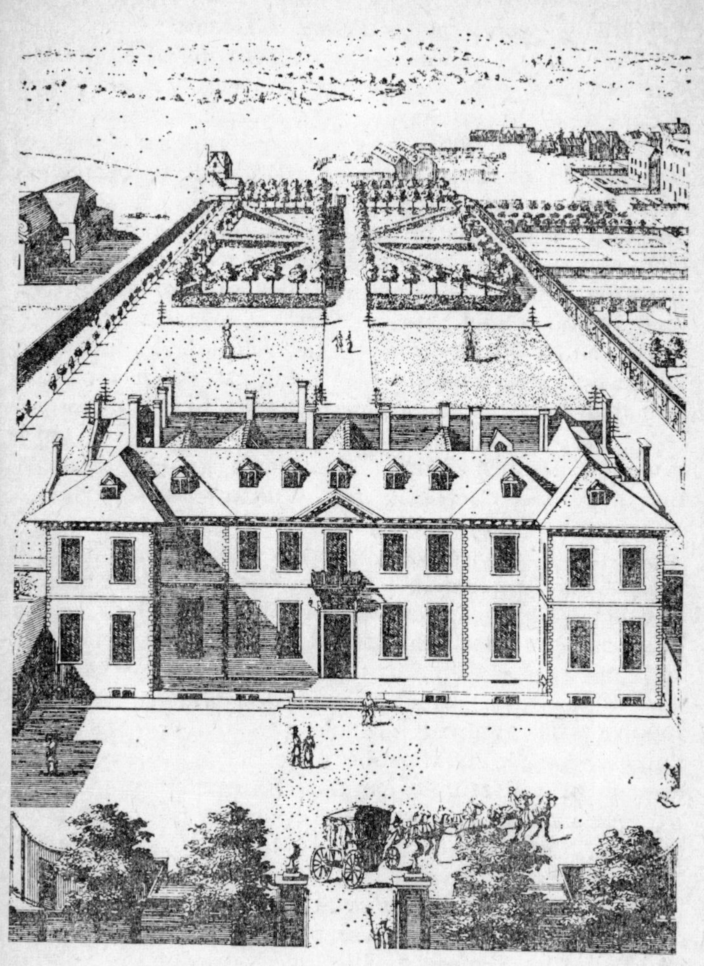

A view of Burlington House, Piccadilly (later the home of the Royal Academy) in about 1720, showing how little the area had been built up at the time.

'Palladians' were James Paine, Giacomo Leoni and William Kent. A central block with a wing at either end was the usual plan, the general aim was symmetry and dignity and the principal guide, Palladio's set of rules. The danger of repetition, of overconformity and lack of invention is obvious, and it was difficult to overcome. After the warmth and richness of Baroque, it was cold and dull-looking. But it was 'correct' and always in good taste and suited to its period, which lasted roughly from 1720 to 1760, when the Adam Brothers brought a new imagination and a lighter touch to the 'classical' style.

Yet one must beware of generalising. To give the impression that nothing was built except in the pure Palladian style between these years would be misleading —for example, Walpole's Strawberry Hill (1747) is a romantic 'Gothick Fancy'. Pure 'classicism' is as alien to the English character as pure Romanticism—a balance between the two is required.

But if the balance was not really found in architecture itself, where the tendency was for one to tip the scales at the expense of the other, we can still nevertheless see the national genius for compromise at work in the churches of James Gibbs. While it is probably true that there are few if any pure Palladian churches, Gibbs more than anyone else attained the elusive balance. His most famous church, St. Martin's-in-the-Fields is 'a combination of Roman temple exterior, a huge steeple, and a baroque interior'. The steeple is perhaps the most interesting. At first glance it is a Wren-style steeple, but a closer inspection reveals a greater 'decorum in its carefully differentiated storeys' which represents, like the rest of the church, a compromise between Baroque 'licence' and Palladian 'propriety'. That this was to be the taste of the time can be seen by the fact that it was frequently imitated; the steeple of St. Giles-in-the-Fields is almost identical, though there an even greater decorum reveals the Palladian leanings of the architect, Henry Flintcroft.

A view of the King's Stables, which formerly stood outside Whitehall Palace. In the background is St. Martin's-in-the-Fields, designed by James Gibbs (1721–26).

William Kent's influence on the Georgian era can hardly be overestimated. A jack of all trades—painter, architect, designer of gardens and furnishing—and master of most, his interest in all forms of design and his emphasis on their interconnection (a completely new idea) undoubtedly helped to spread the good taste of architecture over all aspects of Georgian life.

If to the succeeding generation Kent's interiors seemed too 'heavy', smacking too much of 'external architecture', there is no doubt that his importance as an interior decorator is immense indeed. He was the first to insist that each room should be a work of art on its own; he was also the first to take furniture into account as an essential part of the design of the whole room. Moreover, although Kent's furniture may have seemed 'unnecessarily ponderous' to later designers, when seen in the context of his rooms, it is exactly right. A visit to Holkham Hall in Norfolk, the largest private house in which Kent had a hand, gives an idea of the 'splendour, sumptuousness, rich colours, carving and gilding [which] are the chief ingredients of early Georgian grand interiors', in the design of which no one else could surpass him.

Kent's furniture was massive and ornate: the marble-topped table supported by a huge gilded eagle with a rock in its claws; the velvet-upholstered, richly carved and gilded chair incorporating mythological figures; the enormous eight-foot-high glass-fronted wooden bookcase carved to match the chairs.

As became common practice, Kent's furniture designs were published in the form of a pattern book with measurements scaled down to a size that could be used in houses smaller than the stately mansions they were originally made for.

Queen Anne Furniture

The career of William Kent (1685–1748) spans the reign of Queen Anne and George I. The three names most immediately associated with the Golden Age of English furniture—Chippendale, Hepplewhite and Sheraton—belong to the second half of the century. Only Chippendale can be included in the span of this book. Before considering his work, we must look back over the last decades of the 17th century and the first decades of the 18th century, to which Kent belonged but of which his work was not particularly representative.

At the beginning of our period the chair was little more than a stool with back and arms added; 'back stools' was in fact the name for them. Rigid and high-backed, they were a hangover from Puritanical stiffness. With the accession of William and Mary, a new softening influence from Holland made itself felt—and in the appropriate place. Backs and bottoms sank gratefully into chairs whose comfort surpassed anything so far experienced then (or indeed since). They were equally easy on the eye. Comfort was allied to grace; the chairs felt good and they looked good. The Queen Anne chair, as we now call it, homely yet elegant with its carved back and distinctive cabriole legs, was in fact the typical chair not only of her reign but of the first years of George I's reign. The cabriole leg tended to become shorter and sturdier under George, and to gain the added decoration of a scallop shell. The Queen Anne chair was generally made of walnut. The most important development in furniture-making in the first half of the century was the introduction of mahogany.

Chippendale

Mahogany gave chair designers a new, strong, beautiful material to work with. They seized the opportunity and there followed an extremely inventive period highlighted by Chippendale's *Director*. *The Gentleman's and Cabinet Maker's Director*, to give it its full title, was basically a trade advertisement, but on an unprecedentedly lavish scale. It covered virtually the whole field of furniture-making, and proved so successful that it ran into three editions, the last being almost a different book with 105 new designs. This edition, though it came out in 1762, eight years after the first, shows no great change of furniture style.

What then was the Chippendale style? First, Chippendale's furniture reveals a lessening of the architectural influence seen in Kent's. Further, the classical 'Palladian' style is by no means the basis of his work. It plays a part, but the greater significance of Chippendale's achievement was the introduction from France of the Rococo—a much lighter and more fanciful style. Moreover the influence of the Chinese taste can be seen clearly in his work. The 'Chinese Cabinet'—a room with walls panelled with lacquer and fitted with countless shelves for holding china vases—had already been introduced to cater for the widespread enthusiasm for things Chinese aroused by the ever-expanding Eastern trade.

Consequently furniture makers were familiar with the designs and motifs on Chinese ornaments and welcomed them as a relaxation from the strict discipline of Palladianism. 'Chinese Railing', a type of latticework, was the favourite piece of borrowing, to be seen at its best in Chippendale's latticework chairs.

Classical, Rococo, Chinese—we still haven't exhausted all the aspects of Chippendale's style; there is still the Gothic. This influence is found in the medieval motifs—for example, pointed arcades and tracery—with which he decorated many of his chairs. Gothic tracery can be seen in the bandwork patterns of the splats on Chippendale's most characteristic chair. Working here in one genre, there in another, but more often in a mixture of two or more, the measure of his achievement is that the mingling of influences is seldom obvious, so successfully have they been knitted together to create a new style—that of Chippendale or the *Director*.

Other Furniture

There is no space here to go into all the forms of furniture designed with such care and good taste in the Georgian period, which were 'calculated to improve and refine the present Taste and suited to the Fancy and Circumstances of Persons in all Degrees of life' as Chippendale put it. It is enough to say that beds, bookcases, tables (including card-tables of course), bureaux and such necessities as the gouty or gout stool all bore the marks of superior craftsmanship and tasteful design.

One chair though perhaps deserves a particular mention. New to the Georgian era, still popular enough with us today, the Windsor chair reversed the usual process by evolving in the country and being adopted by the fashionable people up in town; it was understandably popular, since it was both simple and comfortable, in coffee houses and taverns.

China and Glass

Architecture, gardening, furniture, the art of the designer is paramount in all; the same good design informs the smaller things in Georgian life as well. Since drinking occupied a central position in their life, the flourishing of the glass industry comes as no surprise. Glass was no longer for the rich only; good and fairly cheap glasses were available to most people. The Georgian period also saw the introduction of cut glass, brought over from Germany with George I. This led to a new luxury for the upper classes—the chandelier, the development of which offers a history of the changing fashions in miniature—Palladian, Rococo, Chinese.

But alcohol was no longer the only thing drunk. Coffee and especially tea became the craze in the stately home, and the demand for elegant china was great. At first, ladies had to satisfy their 'China Madness' with Dresden ware, but England, late on the scene, finally introduced about 1750 the bone china for which she is still famous today. The discovery at Bow in 1748 that bone ash added to soft paste was more than adequate compensation for the lack of kaolin (the essential ingredient in Dresden ware) produced a china whose hardness and whiteness matched that made in Dresden.

Until that time soft-paste porcelain had been manufactured, notably at Chelsea, where from 1740 onwards some fine free work was produced in a largely French style. Chelsea tureens in the shape of animals and vegetables were popular; so was its flower painting. But it was perhaps most noted for its 'toys' or love tokens, minute scent bottles and patch boxes decorated with cupids and other romantic motifs.

China and earthenware figures too became popular; mythological and pantomime characters and famous actors rubbed shoulders on the mantelpiece. But the great craze for these came just after our period, as did the primacy of Wedgwood and his apprentice, Thomas Turner. The latter, however, may just be mentioned in passing as the probable creator of the ever-popular willow pattern—an English invention and a perfect example of the non-Chinese 'chinoiserie' which, as we have seen, served to soften the outline of a generally 'classical' period.

Literature

The 18th century can be classed as one of the great ages of English literature. A sample list of names is evidence enough: the essayists Addison and Steele; the pamphleteers Defoe and Swift, who also made expeditions into

Jonathan Wild on his way to the gallows in 1725. Wild, a notorious receiver of stolen goods, posed as a zealous 'thief-taker' or arrester of criminals. He was also the subject of a satire by Fielding.

the wider territory of *Robinson Crusoe* and *Gulliver's Travels,* forerunners, in a sense, of the new art form—the novel; and the novelists themselves, Richardson, Fielding, Smollett and Sterne.

But it is perhaps to poetry that we should turn first—to Alexander Pope, whose works, notably *The Essay on Man,* reflect so clearly the mood of the age, the Augustan Age, with its rational intellectual outlook inspired by Newton and firmly established by Locke.

Just as the Palladians turned to Italian architecture for their guide so Pope's *Essay on Criticism* restated the doctrines of the classical school of Italian Renaissance poetry. Thus Pope followed and defined the aims of John Dryden (1631–1700), who first erased the Gothic romantic element from English verse and founded a witty, urbane, civilised style. Civilisation and urbanity—to the Augustan the city was the symbol of man's conquest of the more primitive aspects of nature. Love of the countryside was a mere romantic affectation; the town represented all that was best in man. Thus the subject matter of the poet (sponsored by rich patrons from London society) became town life and public affairs. His role was, in Johnson's words, 'to examine, not the individual but the species: to remark general proportion and large appearances'; his style, in Pope's words, was to give form to 'what oft was thought but ne'er so well expressed'. Polish, urbanity, propriety (preserved if need be by euphemism)—these are the characteristics of the Augustan style, of which Pope was a master. It should also be added that he can be very funny, his wit making the verse light, never 'classically' heavy. Like Chippendale and his followers in furniture, 'it is not a classical temple which Pope has erected in honour of the classics, but a Chinese pagoda bright with shiny tiles and gilded pinnacles'.

This urbane style, written for and about the closed society of the topmost level of London life, was fated to perish by the laws of supply and demand. The new demand came from the growing body of the middle classes. The up-graded professional men, educating themselves with the new circulating libraries and their children at the Dissenting Academies (used because of their higher standard of education by non-Dissenters as well), created a new demand, which turned the poet or author himself into a professional man writing for a mass audience, rather than a patronised mouthpiece for the narrow world of the upper class. As early as 1725 Defoe realised that 'writing is become a very considerable Branch of the English Commerce'. Later, Oliver Goldsmith wrote, 'The author, when unpatronised by the Great, has naturally recourse to the bookseller. There cannot be, perhaps, imagined a combination more prejudicial to taste than this'—to Augustan taste, that is. Yet the poets themselves, Goldsmith (1728–74) with the *Deserted Village,* Thomas Gray (1716–71) with the *Elegy Written in a Country Churchyard,* and William Collins (1721–59) with the *Ode on the popular Superstitions of the Highlands,* reveal a change of direction in subject matter, which stems as much from personal choice as from the demands of the new audience. The Romantic revival was clearly under way by the middle of the century, but the truth is that in poetry, as in the other arts, the undercurrent of Romanticism was never far from the surface throughout the Augustan age. Even the 'public' verse of Pope included personal attacks on individuals, revealing the private emotion threatening to crack the outer veneer.

There is little doubt, however, that the rise of the bookseller and the spread of the printed word hastened the process. We have already seen how the beginning of the 18th century marked the beginning of the newspaper industry, and it is here, in the newspapers and journals, that the new status of the writer is first seen. Joseph Addison and Richard Steele created for their journals

The Tatler and *The Spectator* a new literary form—the periodical essay. The idea behind it was to bring 'philosophy out of closets and libraries . . . to dwell in clubs and assemblies, at tea-tables and in coffee-houses'. They were didactic then, and the people at whom their writing was aimed was the *nouveau riche* business man. But they were light and humorous and some of the regular characters they wrote about, like Addison's Sir Roger de Coverley, are as vivid and amusing to us now as they were then.

In 1731 a more modern type of magazine made its appearance. This was *The Gentleman's Magazine*. On the staff of the publishers was Samuel Johnson, and it is Johnson who affords us the best example of the literary men of the mid-century, depending not so much on patronage as on commissions from booksellers. Arriving in London knowing nobody, he looked first for a patron; then, having failed to find one, turned himself into the dominant literary figure of his time by means of hack-writing of every variety: translations, prefaces, abridgements, 'ghosting' for other writers, magazine articles and poems. It was his *Dictionary* which finally made his name, but his lasting fame probably depends as much on his biographer, James Boswell, as on his own books or journals. Boswell's *Life of Johnson* gives us a clear picture of the man, his circle of friends and the literary life of his age. It describes the frequenters of the coffee house and club, especially in and around Fleet Street, the home of the booksellers and publishers—and incidentally the home of Johnson himself, during the time he was compiling his *Dictionary*. His house, 17 Gough Square, just off Fleet Street, still survives, preserved as a museum.

Daniel Defoe and Jonathan Swift can perhaps be linked together here as pamphleteers and journalists who also produced 'near-novels'. (There is no other similarity however, between Defoe the eagle-eyed observer and

An engraving of Dr Samuel Johnson, perhaps 18th-century London's most celebrated literary figure.

Swift the savage satirist.) *Robinson Crusoe, Moll Flanders,* both by Defoe, and Swift's *Gulliver's Travels* have nearly every attribute of the novel except the author's intention to produce such a form. *Crusoe* was an imaginary autobiography, *Gulliver* a satirical allegory.

By the middle of the century the novel had come into its own with Samuel Richardson's *Pamela* and *Clarissa,* Henry Fielding's *Tom Jones* and *Joseph Andrews* and Tobias Smollett's *Roderick Random* and *Peregrine Pickle.* By the last year of our period, 1760, the time was already ripe, or so it seemed to Lawrence Sterne, for the appearance of the first anti-novel, *Tristram Shandy.*

The titles of all these (and the two forerunners *Crusoe* and *Gulliver*) are revealing; they bear the names of their central character. This demonstrates not so much laziness on the part of the author as an overwhelming interest in character for its own sake, 'that obsession to impart character', which Virginia Woolf defined as the distinguishing mark of the novelist. This is truest, perhaps, of Richardson and Fielding, whose works of character analysis are firmly integrated with a detailed plot ranging over the contemporary scene; Smollett's work has a more picturesque evocation of nature. But the impetus provided by three such diverse talents all working at much the same time established the novel once and for all as a major art form.

Drama

The Georgian period, perhaps because of the spread of the printed word in magazine and novel, was no great age of drama. Society frequented the theatres, but rather in the way that they frequented the public gardens. Being seen there was as important as seeing the play, and since the best boxes were actually on the stage, it was easy to be conspicuous.

However, thanks to one of the great names in the theatre, David Garrick, some advances were made.

The Drury Lane Theatre, one of the two theatres officially allowed in the early 18th century. Here Garrick made his name.

Garrick first made his name in one of the little unlicensed theatres that sprang up. (Only two theatres, Drury Lane and Covent Garden, were officially permitted, as a result of a hangover of puritanical prejudice against the theatre and its practitioners.) He then rose to playing Shakespeare in Drury Lane itself, which was rebuilt to a different plan, which involved clearing the spectators off the stage. By the end of the Georgian period going to the play or show had become a much more 'popular' entertainment, and hundreds of theatres sprang up all over the country, encouraged by the new habit of stars such as Mrs Siddons deigning to tour the provinces. In London in the Vanbrugh-designed Theatre Royal, Haymarket, John Rich drew in the wider public with his invention of the English pantomime. The anglicised versions of Harlequin and Pantaloon delighted the audiences, as did John Gay's musical portrait of London's underworld, *The Beggar's Opera,* produced at the theatre in 1727.

Plays of the first half of the century are seldom performed now, yet strangely enough, as this book is being written, two of them, Vanbrugh's *The Relapse, or Virtue in Danger* and John Gay's musical play, *The Beggar's Opera* are appearing successfully in London's West End.

Music

It is perhaps true to say that the Georgians loved musicians more than they loved music. Certainly the works themselves appeared secondary to the singer or conductor who performed them and the composer who created them. Rival factions formed around rival singers, most of whom were foreign; English artists and composers were generally ignored.

The greatest name in English music at this time was a German, George Frederick Handel, brought over to this country by George I. Handel lost George II's favour by writing an anthem for the Prince of Wales, who was loathed by his father, but he regained it with the *Messiah* which impressed the king so much he rose to his feet at the Hallelujah Chorus, a custom which persists to this day. In 1740 *Rule Britannia* was first played, with immediate success. During the Seven Years War this tune by Dr Arne became a second national anthem.

A slightly strange musical footnote considering the disgusting state of the Thames at that time, is provided by Handel's *Water Music*, inspired by the river but probably also owing something to such entertainments on water as the ice fairs and the Lord Mayor's Show.

Art

Painting, like music, was foreign-dominated. This was largely the result of the Grand Tour—the visit, guided by a private tutor, to the 'classical' lands, especially Italy, which was the *sine qua non* of the young aristocrat's education. But gradually the English portrait and landscape painters came into their own, aided in no small measure by the foundation of the Royal Academy of Arts in 1768, with Sir Joshua Reynolds as its first president. (Now housed in Old Burlington House in Piccadilly, the Royal Academy was originally in Pall Mall.) This was an offshoot of a club, the Society of Incorporated Artists, for artists whose interest was in drawing from life. The Royal Academy held its first exhibition in 1769 and had an immediate success.

The artist most closely connected with our period, however, is William Hogarth. Hogarth was a painter with a conscience; as much as anyone else in the first half of the century he pointed an accusing finger at the false standards of the upper class, its looseness of morals, its extravagances, and its wilful ignorance of the degraded life of the poor. Hazlitt said of him, 'he never looks at any object but to find a moral or ludicrous effect', and while this is to ignore the humane and sympathetic side of Hogarth, which does appear in his work, there is no doubt that art for art's sake, accurate reproduction by itself, was anathema to him. Consequently, he is often careless of draughtsmanship, but this is a small defect in works of such power, honesty and originality. As Horace Walpole said, 'Hogarth had no model to follow and improve upon. He created his art, and used colours instead of language. Sometimes he ran to tragedy, not in the catastrophe of kings and heroes, but in marking how vice conducts insensibly and incidentally to misery and shame'. A fair assessment of Hogarth's documentary criticism can be gained from his series of pictures, *Marriage à la Mode* and *The Rake's Progress*, or from single subjects like *Gin Lane* and *Beer Alley*. We have witnessed the birth of the newspaper; with Hogarth we see the birth of the newspaper cartoonist.

Places to See

West End

As an area of 18th-century expansion, the West End (W.1) is still full of buildings of the period. To take a few examples: in Grafton Street, off Bond Street, there is a row of mansions thought to have been built by Sir Robert Taylor in 1750. Crewe House, 32 Curzon Street (off Park Lane) was built by Edward Shepherd in 1735, but it has been restored since. Another of Shepherd's ventures is Shepherd Market (1735), off Curzon Street. It is sited on the spot where the May Fair used to be held. No. 44 Berkeley Square is one of the few houses designed by William Kent (1744). Nos. 6, 7 and 18 Clifford Street, off New Bond Street, were built in 1720 and are fine examples of Georgian building. No. 24 Hanover Square, off south side of Oxford Street, is one of the houses built when the square was laid out in 1717, and in Cavendish Square (off north side of Oxford Street) some of the original houses remain. Further south, in Soho, there is an early 18th-century terrace in Broadwick Street, off Berwick Street, and in Meard Street (off Wardour Street) there are some less grand houses (1732) than some of those already mentioned.

In Piccadilly there is an eye-catching archway leading into a quadrangle flanked by Old Burlington House, rebuilt in 1715. It now houses the Royal Academy of Arts, originally centred in Pall Mall. The Society of Antiquaries in London, founded in 1707, is based in the west wing. Sotheby's, the most celebrated of salerooms, founded in 1714, is at 34 Old Bond Street. The West End branch of the Royal Bank of Scotland is housed in what was formerly Queensborough House (built by Giacomo Leoni in 1721) at the corner of Savile Row. Another reminder of the time is the statue of George II in Golden Square.

Whitehall, Westminster and St. James's

Whitehall was the name of the Stuarts' royal palace, of which little now remains apart from the Banqueting Hall on the east side of the street. The Telephone Exchange in Craig's Court has a 1700 façade and of the two Admiralty buildings, the older dates from 1723–6; it was designed by Thomas Ripley. Beyond the Admiralty in Whitehall but on the same side is the Horse Guards, famous for its clock tower by Kent and John Vardy (1742–52).

Among Georgian streets in Westminster is Queen Anne's Gate (off Tothill Street). This is a small close built in 1704 by William Patterson and includes some fine examples of domestic architecture. Another is Great College Street (off Millbank), which includes on its north side a terrace of 18th-century houses. Also of interest is that No. 10 Downing Street was given to Sir Robert Walpole by George II in 1732. In 1698 Wren was made surveyor of Westminster Abbey and proceeded to build up the central tower and design two others for the west end of the abbey. Hawksmoor later realised these designs. (Wren's plan of the abbey can be seen in the Abbey Museum.)

In the area of St. James's, places of Georgian interest include Pickering Place (off St. James's Street). The approach to this tiny square, containing good examples of Georgian houses, is lined with dark oak. In the middle of the square stands a sundial with 'William Pickering fundator 1710' inscribed on it. Two shops dating from the period are Berry's, the wine merchants, at No. 3 St. James's Street and Fribourg & Treyer's, built in 1720, formerly a snuff shop, now a tobacconist, at the top of Haymarket. Also worth noting is the equestrian statue of William III in St. James's Square.

Holborn and the City

Coram's Fields is now a children's playground in Guilford Street, which runs off Gray's Inn Road. In 1724 the Foundling Hospital was built on this site and remained there until 1926. The offices at 40 Brunswick Square have many relics of the former building on show to the public (admission free; Mondays and Fridays 10 am—12 pm, 2—4 pm). Further east, 42 Hart Street is a fine house dating from the early years of the 18th century. (Hart Street is off Mark Lane, which runs between Great Tower Street and Fenchurch Street.) No. 61 Hopton Street (running off Bankside) is another isolated early 18th-century house.

Greenwich

The Royal Naval College was first completed by Wren in 1705 as a hospital for disabled sailors. Only the chapel and the Painted Hall (with ceiling paintings by Sir James Thornhill) are open to the public. On the east side of Greenwich Park on the top of Maze Hill is Vanbrugh Castle, built by Vanbrugh for himself; it is now a R.A.F. Memorial School. Near the west gate of the park is Meartney House (built in 1694) inhabited by General Wolfe. Crooms Hill, running along the west side of the park, includes some late 17th- and early 18th-century houses, among them the Manor House (1697).

Hampstead

There are many beautiful Georgian buildings in this area, for example, in Hampstead High Street, where some 18th-century houses are perhaps at first unrecognisable because of modern shop fronts. Church Row, which runs off the High Street and comprises terraces of houses, is one of the finest surviving Georgian streets. Fenton House in Hampstead Grove is an example of a 1693 mansion. It is open to the public on weekdays (not Tuesday) from

10 am—1 pm, 2 pm—5 pm; Sunday 2 pm—5 pm; admission 2s. 6d. Items include notable pieces of furniture and porcelain and among the many musical instruments is a harpsichord used by Handel.

Chelsea

In Chelsea good examples of Georgian houses can be found in Cheyne Walk (a continuation westwards of the Chelsea Embankment) and in Cheyne Row, running off Cheyne Walk. No. 215 King's Road was built in 1720 and Argyll House in 1723 by Giacomo Leoni.

Hammersmith

The Upper Mall runs along the river and contains some fine Georgian domestic architecture, including Sussex House (1726). Hammersmith Terrace, also overlooking the river, was built in 1750.

Chiswick

In Chiswick is Hogarth's House, Hogarth Lane. It was his summer residence from 1749 to 1764 and has since been restored. (Open to the public, admission 1s., weekdays 11 am—4 pm; Sunday 2—4 pm.) Chiswick House, whose gardens are now a public park, was built in 1725–27 by the 3rd Earl of Burlington. (Open to the public from April to September every day 10.30 am—5.30 pm and from Wednesday to Sunday from October to March, 10.30 am—4 pm. Admission 1s. 6d.)

Museums to Visit

British Museum

The British Museum itself has Georgian connections, since it was founded in 1753 to house the Cottonian Library and later, a large collection of works of art and antiquities of Sir Hans Sloane and some manuscripts collected by Robert Harley. These were moved to Montague House after it was bought in 1755 with money raised by a public lottery. In 1757 George II presented the Royal Library to the museum and finally in 1759, it was opened to the public. Since then a new and bigger building has been built on the same site to replace Montague House.

In Bays XVIII–XX of the King Edward Gallery are 18th-century examples of glass, porcelain and watches.

Address:	Great Russell Street, W.C.1
Admission:	Free
Opening hours:	Monday—Saturday: 10 am—5 pm Sunday: 2.30 pm—6 pm
Closed:	Christmas Day and Good Friday Open Bank Holidays usual hours
Access:	

By Underground:

Tottenham Court Road (Central and Northern lines). Turn right along Tottenham Court Road and right at Great Russell Street. Museum on left.

Russell Square (Piccadilly Line). Left out of station, cross Russell Square, and left down Montague Street to Great Russell Street and main entrance of Museum.

By Bus:

77, 68, 188, 196 to Southampton Row. Turn left along Great Russell Street.

73 to Tottenham Court Road/Oxford Street. Right along Great Russell Street.

7, 8, 22, 23, 25, from Holborn direction. Alight at High Holborn, just past Kingsway, and cross road, along Drury Lane or Grape Street, cross New Oxford Street and continue along Coptic Street or Museum Street.

By Car:

Drive from West along Oxford Street, turn left at Tottenham Court Road, and right almost immediately at Great Russell Street.

From East, along Holborn to Kingsway, turn right along Southampton Row, and left at Great Russell Street.

N.B. There is limited parking at the Museum; otherwise, at side in Montague Street/Russell Square.

Guildhall Museum

The museum has a fine collection of London antiquities, including pipes, ranging from the 18th to the 19th century, gloves, ranging over approximately the same periods, and 16th- to 18th-century glass etc. Relevant specifically to our period are a whipping-post and manacles from Newgate prison and the sign from the Boar's Head tavern in Eastcheap. Guildhall Museum also houses the Museum of Leathercraft illustrating that craft in this and many other periods.

Address:	On Bassishaw High Walk, up stairs by Gillette House in Basinghall Street, overlooking London Wall, E.C.2
Admission:	Free
Opening hours:	Monday—Saturday: 10 am—5 pm
Closed:	Sundays, Bank Holidays

Access:

By Underground:

Aldersgate (Metropolitan or Circle lines). Turn right out of station along Aldersgate as far as London Wall. Turn left, and the museum is up on the high walkway opposite ruin of church tower.

St. Paul's (Central Line). Walk along Cheapside to Wood Street, left to Gresham Street, right for one block to Aldermanbury. Up stairs on right at end before junction with London Wall.

Moorgate (Metropolitan and Northern lines). Turn right along Moorgate, to London Wall. Turn right.

Bank (Central Line). Go along Princes Street at side of Bank of England to Gresham Street. Left as far as Basinghall Street. Right. Museum at far end of Basinghall Street up steps by Gillette House.

By Bus:

7, 8, 22, 23, 25, to St. Paul's end of Cheapside, then follow instructions given under St. Paul's Underground Station above.

76, 43, 21, 11, 9, 141, to London Wall/Moorgate. Follow instructions as from Moorgate Station.

By Car:

Parking is difficult except at weekends out of 'meter' hours. No parking at any time on London Wall.

From East: drive to the Bank then along Princes Street by Bank of England, turn left at Gresham Street, and right at Aldermanbury.

From West: Holborn/Newgate Street, turn left at Aldersgate and right at Gresham Street. Park in area behind Guildhall.

Kensington Palace

The State Apartments comprise several rooms designed by or containing items by Christopher Wren and William Kent:

The Queen's Staircase: designed by Wren in 1690.

The Queen's Bedroom: contains a desk of the second half of the 17th century.

Queen's Drawing Room: decorated by Kent in 1724. It looks over a court to a gatetower by Wren.

Cupola Room: contains a clock, 'Temple of Four Monarchies', made around 1730.

King William's Gallery: designed in 1694 by Wren, with wood carving typical of the Georgian period. The ceiling was painted by Kent in 1725.

King's Staircase: partly designed by Wren. Kent painted the walls to look like a gallery.

Presence Chamber: Kent painted the ceiling; Grinling Gibbons executed the limewood carving over the mantel.

Address:	Kensington Gardens, W.8
Admission:	Free
Opening hours:	Monday—Saturday: 10 am—6 pm 10 am—4 pm (October—February) Sunday: 2 pm—4 pm
Closed:	Christmas Day, Good Friday

Access:

By Underground:

Queensway (Central Line). Cross Bayswater Road and walk through Broad Walk in Kensington Gardens to Palace.

Kensington High Street (Circle or District lines from Earls Court to Edgware Road). Turn right along Kensington High Street to Park. Left through Park to Palace.

By Bus:

12, 88 along Bayswater Road to Queensway, then as above from Queensway Station.

9, 46, 52, 73, to Palace Gate in Kensington Road. Walk through Park to Palace.

By Car:

The best place to park is in the squares and side streets off Bayswater Road or Kensington Road. Then walk through Park.

The London Museum

This museum is based at Kensington Palace and illustrates London life through its multiple stages—Georgian period included. (Anything not on view can be seen on request to the Director.)

Rooms 17–20 are the most relevant to our period. Among the items represented arc the works of contemporary craftsmen: jewellery and watches, silver, small arms, glassware and the famous Chelsea porcelain. You can also see an example of a Georgian shop front and examples of old shop signs. Room 18 contains an 18th-century bedroom with the bed in which the Old Pretender was born (1688).

Admission and access details as for Kensington Palace.

The National Maritime Museum

This museum at Greenwich offers reminders of the history of the sea and some examples relating to the Georgian period can be seen there. The Museum is laid out chronologically, and the first part of our period is represented in Queen's House and the second half in the Caird Galleries by contemporary seascapes and relics. In the Barge House you can see the shallop (1689) of Mary II and a state barge built in 1732 for Frederick, Prince of Wales.

Address:	Greenwich, S.E.10
Admission:	Free
Opening hours:	Monday—Saturday: 10 am—6 pm
	Sunday: 2.30 pm—6 pm
Closed:	Christmas Day, Good Friday

Access:

By Southern Region:

From Charing Cross, Waterloo or London Bridge.
Best stop is Maze Hill. From station cross Maze Hill to

Park Vista directly opposite. Museum is on the left at the end of this road.

By Bus:

70, 188, 53, 163, 177 to Greenwich. The museum is behind Romney Road on the right, before it becomes Trafalgar Road.

Victoria and Albert Museum

Some Chelsea porcelain may be seen in Rooms 6–7 though this room deals mainly with miscellaneous items. Eighteenth-century costumes can be seen among the large collection in room 40—the Octagon Court—and at the south entrance to this court stands L. F. Roubilliac's statue of Handel (1735), which stood originally in Vauxhall Gardens.

Examples of English decor popular at the time of William and Mary are in room 56, a panelled room from Clifford's Inn (1686–8) and noteworthy examples of furniture. Rooms 57 and 58 deal with most of the remainder of our period (1700–50). They contain typical rooms, one designed by James Gibbs.

In room 121 is some more china of the first half of the 18th century and to give you a glimpse of things at the very end of our period, there is a room of 1760. Room 63 exhibits a carved marble fireplace (1750) taken from Northumberland House.

Address:	South Kensington, S.W.7
Admission:	Free
Opening hours:	Monday—Saturday: 10 am—6 pm
	Sunday: 2.30 pm—6 pm
Closed:	Christmas Day and Good Friday
	Open Bank Holidays usual hours

Access:

By Underground:

South Kensington (District, Circle and Piccadilly lines). A

subway connects the station and the museum, coming out on the north-west (Exhibition Road) side. Main entrance to museum is on Cromwell Road.

By Bus:

207, 45, 49 to South Kensington Station.
14, 30, 74 to Brompton Oratory, at junction of Brompton Road and Cromwell Road.

National Portrait Gallery

Portraits of many Georgian celebrities are on view in this gallery. William and Mary, and Queen Anne are in Room 11 and their successors, George I and II can be seen in Room 6 along with some of the famous generals and statesmen, for example, General Wolfe and William Pitt. In this room there is also a bust of Sir Robert Walpole, done by Rysbrack. Portraits of 42 members of the Kit Kat Club are hung in Rooms 2 and 3, while in Room 1 there are pictures of 18th-century literary men and artists. Rooms 4 and 5 contain pictures of other well-known figures, for example, John Wesley and Horace Walpole. Here there also hang pictures of Dr Johnson and his circle.

Address:	2 St. Martin's Place, W.C.2
Admission:	Free
Opening hours:	Monday—Friday: 10 am—5 pm Saturday: 10 am—6 pm Sunday and Boxing Day: 2 pm—6 pm
Closed:	Good Friday, Christmas Day and Christmas Eve

N.B. Lectures on Saturdays at 3.15 in October—March.

Access:

By Underground:

Trafalgar Square (Bakerloo Line).
Leicester Square (Northern and Piccadilly lines).
Walk down to the end of Charing Cross Road. The

Gallery is at the foot on the right, where Charing Cross Road joins St. Martin's Lane.

By Bus:

1, 24, 29, 127, 134, 163, 176 to lower part of Charing Cross Road. Proceed as for Leicester Square. Buses from all directions going to Trafalgar Square. Proceed to north side of the Square and go left into St. Martin's Lane.

National Gallery

Here there are pictures by the Georgian painter, Hogarth, to be found in the English Room, Room XVI.

Address:	Trafalgar Square, W.C.2
Admission:	Free
Opening hours:	Monday—Saturday: 10 am—6 pm Tuesday and Thursday: 10 am—9 pm in summer
Closed:	Good Friday, Christmas Eve and Christmas Day

Access:

By Underground:

Trafalgar Square and Leicester Square as for National Portrait Gallery.
Charing Cross (District, Circle, Bakerloo and Northern lines). Come out of station into Villiers Street, turn left at top on to the Strand. Carry along the Strand to Trafalgar Square. The gallery is on the north side of the square.

By Bus:

Buses from all directions to Trafalgar Square.

Dr Johnson's House

This is worth a visit to see relics of the man himself and also to have an interior view of a typical Georgian house.

Address:	17 Gough Square, E.C.4
Admission:	2s.
Opening hours:	Weekdays: 10.30 am—5 pm
	October—April: 10.30 am—4 pm
Closed:	Bank Holidays

Access:

By Bus:

4A, 6, 9, 11, 13, 15, to Fleet Street. Gough Square is on the left going towards St. Paul's, the stop just after Fetter Lane, also on the left.

John Wesley's House

This is also open to the public and is another example of Georgian interiors; it exhibits personal mementoes of the founder of Methodism. Wesley's Chapel, built later, retains Wesley's pulpit, and there is a statue of Wesley in front of the chapel and his grave behind.

Address:	47 City Road, E.C.1
Admission:	1s.
Opening hours:	Weekdays: 10 am—1 pm; 2 pm—4 pm

Access:

By Underground:

Moorgate (Metropolitan, Circle and Northern lines). Turn left out of station up Moorgate towards City Road. The house and chapel are on the right, not far up.
Bank (Central Line). Come out at Princes Street, continue along it to Moorgate, and from thence to City Road.

Old Street (Northern Line). Come out of station and turn left down City Road to the House which is on the left.

By Bus:

9, 11, 133, 21, 76, to Moorgate. Proceed as for underground. 43, 104, 141, 214, 239, to City Road. Get off at junction with Epworth Street.

Who's Who in Georgian London

Anne: Reigned 1702–14. Often unwell, Anne was uninterested in court life, preferring Kensington and Bath to St. James's. She was dominated by female favourites, including Sarah, Duchess of Marlborough.

Chippendale, Thomas (1718–89): cabinet-maker whose furniture, notably his chairs, began a great age of furniture design.

Defoe, Daniel (1661–1731): tradesman and writer of pamphlets, notably *A Tour through Great Britain,* and of the 'novel' *Robinson Crusoe.*

Fielding, Henry (1707–54): novelist and magistrate, author of *Tom Jones* and campaigner against crime and corruption.

George I: Reigned 1714–27. First of the Hanoverian line, he was more interested in Hanover than in England. As a result many prerogatives of the crown passed to the Whig chiefs.

George II: Reigned 1727–60. Ruled under the thumb of his wife Caroline and her favourite, Sir Robert Walpole, often known as England's first 'Prime Minister'.

Handel, George Frederick (1685–1759): Composer who came to London with George I and wrote some of his greatest works here, including *The Water Music* and the *Messiah.*

Hogarth, William (1697–1764): artist whose mordant portrayal of social conditions set the style for later cartoonists and helped to bring about the reform of London life.

Johnson, Samuel (1709–84): great literary figure of mid-18th-century London; hack writer, poet and book compiler, famous for his *Dictionary*, his *Rambler* magazine and his literary circle.

Pope, Alexander (1688–1744): major poet of the Augustan age; writer of polished witty verse, notable for its epigrammatic epic style.

William and Mary: Reigned 1688–1702. Invited to replace the tyrannical Roman Catholic James II; their accession assured the trend towards religious toleration, parliamentary supremacy and the maintenance of civil liberty.

Wren, Christopher (1632–1723): great architect who after the Great Fire of 1666 changed the face of London with his 'Queen Anne' houses and his City churches, notably St. Paul's Cathedral.

Further Reading List

Bernard Ash	*The Golden City*, Phoenix House
Elizabeth Burton	*The Georgians at Home*, Longmans, Green
George E. Eades	*Historic London, the story of a city and its people*, Queen Anne Press
M. Dorothy George	*London Life in the Eighteenth Century*, Penguin Books
John Gloag	*Georgian Grace*, Adam and Charles Black
O. and N. Hamilton	*Royal Greenwich*, Greenwich Bookshop
Michael Harrison	*London Growing: The Development of a Metropolis*, Hutchinson
R. J. Mitchell and M. D. R. Leys	*A History of London Life*, Longmans, Green
E. N. Williams	*Life in Georgian England*, Batsford
John Peneyre and Michael Ryan	*The Observer's Book of Architecture*, Frederick Warne
Marjorie & D. H. B. Quennell	*A History of Everyday Things in England*, volume II, Batsford Ltd.
G. M. Trevelyan	*English Social History*, Longmans, Green
T. W. West	*A History of Architecture in England*, University of London Press
R. J. White	*A Short History of England*, Cambridge at the University Press
E. L. Woodward	*History of England*, Methuen

Discovering London

Other Books in the Series

This volume is one of a set of eight books that trace the growth of London from Roman times to the end of Queen Victoria's reign. The other books are:

Set One

1. *Roman London* by Grace Derwent
2. *The Conqueror's London* by Derek Brechin
3. *Medieval London* by Kenneth Derwent
4. *Tudor London* by A. G. Robertson

Set Two

5. *Stuart London* by Malpas Pearse
6. This book
7. *Regency London* by Douglas Hill
8. *Victorian London* by Graham Norton

Each title is available separately, price 6s. Alternatively each set of four volumes is available in a box with a fold-out map of the area, price 25s.